# J.-P. Benamou

C000156651

# NORMANL _ _ _ _

# An illustrated Field-Guide

## 7 June to 22 August 1944

# EDITIONS HEIMDAL

Château de Damigny   F-14400 BAYEUX

# SUMMARY

## A. British Sector

## B. American Sector

## C. The Falaise Pockett

*Translated by G. Lecourt and Anthony Whilley.*

Copyright Heimdal, 1982.

# FOREWORD

On the evening of 6 June 1944 the allied armies won a glorious victory in the battle of the beaches, the first phase of the allied plan for the liberation of Europe from the north-west, Operation Overlord.

With the loss of 9000 men, of whom nearly 3000 were killed, 135,000 men disembarked on Tuesday, 6 June. They held a portion of French territory which varied in depth from a few hundred metres painfully clawed from the Germans to a few kilometres. It extended in all along 80 kilometres of the Normandy coast and it was absolutely essential to secure and consolidate the position before advancing further.

This first spectacular victory on the beaches was the result of aerial supremacy, surprise in the choice of a landing place, and the high training of resolute and very well equipped men.

The second phase of Operation Overlord, which became known as the "Battle of Normandy", has not been crowned with the same prestige as D-Day. After 77 days of a war of attrition on two fronts, the campaign in Normandy became the Battle for France where the rapid successes of the Allies presaged the final outcome of the war in Europe.

The account of D-Day is clearly set out in a number of international works and is well illustrated in the museums on the coast of Lower Normandy (see map). The history of the campaign in Normandy (7 June - 21 August 1944) because of its intricacy remains complex and fragmentary even today. I have based my account on the contents of the battle plan of General B.L. Montgomery as it took shape in the events which unfolded in the development of the campaign, and the account is illustrated by many contemporary photographs. The Memorial Museum of the Battle of Normandy at Bayeux complements this account as it displays a number of documents and realia relating to this campaign. Together, the present guide and the Museum at Bayeux should allow visitors to Lower Normandy interested in history to relive this campaign with its many military operations. This book presents the topography and history of the campaign and lists the memorials which can still be seen : military cemeteries, monuments and stones which honour the deeds and sacrifice of tens of thousands of men who are recalled by the objects and documents preserved in the Museum at Bayeux.

**J. P. BENAMOU**

## THE DIFFERENT SECTORS FROM EAST TO WEST.

### A. The British Sector.

It stretches between the Rivers Touque and Drôme, or from Bois de Bavent (North east of Caen) to Port-en-Bessin. There we find the 2nd British Army (General Miles Dempsey) reinforced on July 23 by the 1st Canadian Army (General Crerar), both under the command of the 21st Army Group (General B.L. Montgomery).

### B. The American Sector.

It stretches from the River Drôme to the west coast of Cotentin peninsula. Until July 30 it contains the 1st US Army under General Bradley. On July 31 it is reinforced by the 3rd US Army (General Patton); General Hodges then takes over control of the 1st US Army while General Bradley assumes overall control of the 12th US Army Group. General Bradley receives his orders from General Montgomery until the end of August; he in turn is under the juridiction of the supreme commander of the allied expeditionary forces, the American General, Dwight D. Eisenhower (see chart).

We have tried to follow a chronological order of events in 14 chapters ending with the annihilation of the German Army in the Falaise pocket.

### A. In the British Sector.

A-1. The Bridgehead of the airborne troops on the River Orne from 7.6 to 17.8.44.

A-2. The installation of the troops of the 2nd British Army and the Canadian front from 7.6 to 8.7.44.

A-3. The battle for Tilly, from 7.6 to 25.6.44.

A-4. The battle in the Odon valley. Operations Epsom and Jupiter from 24.6 to 25.7.44.

A-5. The capture of Caen. Operations Charnwood and Atlantic from 8 to 18 July 1944.

A-6. The failure of British armour in the plain of Caen. Operations Goodwood and Spring. 18-28 July 1944.

A-7. The breakthrough in the Bocage; Operation Bluecoat from 31.7 to 12.8.44.

A-8. The Canadian push towards Falaise: Operations Totalize and Tractable 7 to 16 August 1944.

### B. In the American Sector.

B-1. The installation of the 1st US Army from Omaha Beach to the bridgehead of the airborne troops in Cotentin: 7.6 to 16.6.1944.

B-2. The battle for the Cotentin peninsula. The siege and the capture of Cherbourg from 18 to 26 June 1944.

B-3. The Hedgerows War from La-Haye-du-Puits to Saint-Lô 26.6 to 18.7.1944.

B-4. The breakthrough then the rush on of the Americans west of Saint-Lô: Operation Cobra from 24.7 to 1.8.1944.

B-5. The American exploitation of Operation Cobra and the German counter-attack at Mortain: Operation Liege, from 2.8 to 12.8.1944.

B-6. The chase and the German retreat in the Mortain-Argentan pocket.

### C. The end of the battle of Normandy in the Falaise pocket, 17 to 22 August 1944.

## THE PLAN OF THE BATTLE OF NORMANDY AS IMAGINED AND REALISED BY GENERAL MONTGOMERY.

First it was essential to establish a strong bridgehead behind the front-line troops so that they would always maintain the initiative in the fighting. Then, when supplies and reinforcements were completely assured, the master plan was to draw in as many German troops and as much armour as possible on the east flank in the sector of the 2nd British Army under General Dempsey around Caen, to allow the 1st American Army of General Bradley to break through and move south across a weakened German line. The English and Canadians would seek to attract German attention by constantly attacking the important crossroads of Caen and the plain beyond, opening the road to Paris. The German High Command considered this sector as the most dangerous and would throw in the bulk of the German forces there neglecting the American sector which was more distant. Besides, the Germans did not think much of the Americans whom they saw as cowboys far from their homes and with little motivation for a war of attrition, 5000 kilometres from their homeland.

Once the breakthrough had been made by the American 1st Army, the 3rd US Army of General Patton would rush into the gap thundering down to Brittany, reaching the Loire and then turning towards the River Seine. It would be backed up in the east by the 1st US Army in a turning movement having Caen as a centre. The River Seine should be reached on D + 90, trapping and destroying a large part of the German forces in the west. To carry out this clever plan, Montgomery deliberately gave the most unpleasant and the most dangerous part to the English and Canadian soldiers whose valour he knew so well. The spectacular advance was reserved for the Americans who won the title of "liberators" almost exclusively.

Commandement allié du 6/6 au 23/7/44

21ème Groupe d'Armées Britannique
général B.L. Montgomery

1ère Armée US
Lt. Gal.O.N. Bradley

2ème Armée Brit.
Lt. Gal Sir M.Dempsey

| Vème Corps | VIIème Corps | VIIIème Corps | XIXème Corps |
|---|---|---|---|
| Gerow | Collins | Middleton | Corlett |

| Ier Corps | VIIIème Corps | XIIème Corps | XXXe Corps |
|---|---|---|---|
| Crocker | O'Connor | Ritchie | Bucknall |

Commandement allié du 31/7 au 25/8/44

21ème Groupe d'Armées Britannique
Gal. B.L. Montgomery

1ère Armée Us
Lt.Gl.Hodges

Ve Corps
Maj.Gal.Gerow

3e Armée Us
Lt.Gl.Patton

| VIIe Corps | XIXe Corps | VIIIe Corps | XIIe Corps | XVe Corps | XXe Corps |
|---|---|---|---|---|---|
| Collins | Corlett | Middleton | Cock puis Eddy | Haislip | Walker |

1ère Armée Canadienne
Lt.Gal.H.D.G.Grerar

2ème Armée Brit.
Lt.Gal.Sir Miles Dempsey

| Ier C. Brit. | IIe C. CDN | VIIIe Corps | XIIe Corps | XXXe Corps |
|---|---|---|---|---|
| Crocker | Simonds | O'Connor | Ritchie | Horrocks |

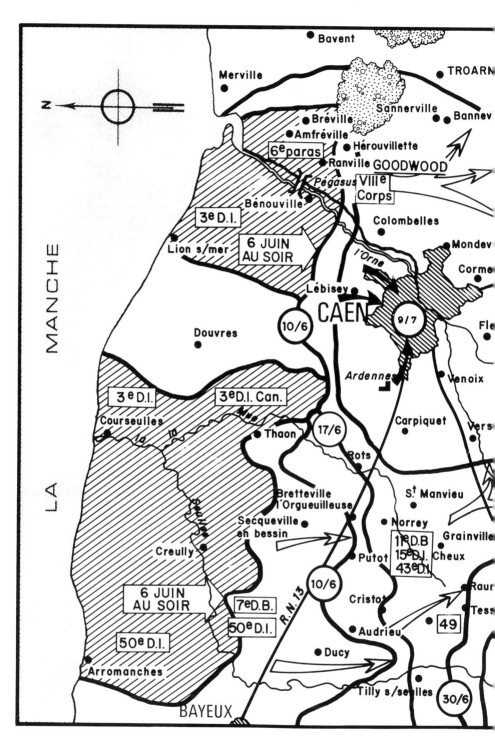

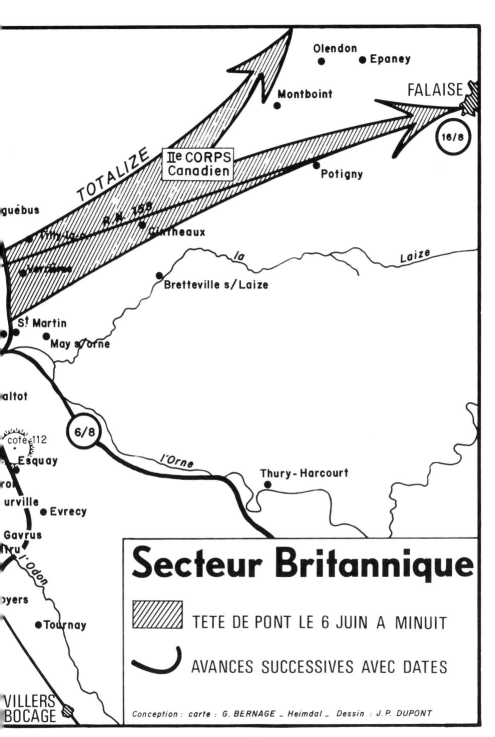

Olendon
Epaney

Montboint

FALAISE

TOTALIZE

IIe CORPS Canadien

Potigny

16/8

guébus

R.N. 158

Tilly la...

Cintheaux

Verrières

la

Laize

Bretteville s/Laize

St Martin

May s/Orne

altot

cote 112

6/8

Esquay

l'Orne

ro

urville

Evrecy

Thury-Harcourt

Gavrus

ru

l'Odon

yers

Tournay

VILLERS
BOCAGE

# Secteur Britannique

TETE DE PONT LE 6 JUIN A MINUIT

AVANCES SUCCESSIVES AVEC DATES

Conception : carte : G. BERNAGE _ Heimdal _ Dessin : J.P. DUPONT

# A. THE BRITISH SECTOR

## A.1. The bridgehead of the Airborne Troops between the Rivers Orne and Dives from June 7 to August 17 1944.

In the evening of June 6th, the 6th Airborne Division of General Gale had taken all its objectives and managed to regroup 75% of its men in a bridgehead east of the canal from Caen to the sea and the River Orne, the centre of which was the village of Ranville where the HQ of the Division was situated.

Two counter-attacks supported by light armoured vehicles had been successfully repelled at Bénouville and Hérouvillette. But the hardest task was still ahead for the allied troops. The Germans would do their utmost to get rid of this wing of the invasion. Holding the two bridges and keeping them was essential.

The 711th German Inf.Div. with its 14,000 men spread along 25 kilometres of coastline east of the River Orne could not do much with its 60 motorised guns and 25 R-35 obsolete French tanks.

Moreover it was mostly horsedrawn.

The 346 th German Inf.Div. situated round the estuary of the River Seine was better equipped and more powerful, for it had motorised artillery.

*Below: A German NCO giving first aid to a British para-trooper (Heimdal coll.) Opposite: The bridge at Ranville, "Pegasus Bridge" on June 8 which allowed the 3rd British Inf.Div. to send ammunitions and supplies to the paratroopers of the 6th Airborne. (I.W.M)*

The 21st *Panzerdivision* (German Armoured Division) whose HQ was in Caen included 3 battalions of grenadiers and several batteries of modern selfpropelled antitank guns. These could intervene directly against the 6th Airborne. The 6th Airborne had a complement of 6,000 men. It was backed by n° 3, 4, 6 Commandos and 45 (RM) of the 1st Special Brigade of General Lord Lovat - about 2500 men, with the one Divisional Armoured Squadron - 16 light Tetrach tanks brought in by gliders and some 20 antitank guns.

In the morning of **June 7**, the British, Canadian and French red and green berets - 177 men in N° 4 Commando were entrenched round the woody hill between Sallenelles and a place north of Troarn. They controlled the plain southwards. In the west they were overlooking Ranville and its familiar steeple. The bridges could be seen beyond. It was the supply route for the neighbouring 3rd British Inf.Division of General Rennie.

In the east the air raids of the previous day had blown up the bridges on the River Dives. It was impossible for the Germans to bring up heavy equipement from that direction through the flooded low ground.

All were getting ready to fulfill the mission assigned them: to protect the right flank of the 2nd British Army which had landed the day before on *Sword,*

*Juno* and *Gold* beaches, and to prevent the Germans from entering the area stretching between the River Orne and the River Dives north of the road Troarn-Sannerville-Colombelles.

During the fighting which followed the parachutists occupied positions which remained practically unchanged until August 17th.

*The situation on June 7th was as follows.*

- The 5th Parachute Brigade controlled the bridges.

- The 3rd Parachute Brigade of General Hill defended the hilly ground with more important groups in keypoints at "Plain", "Mesnil" crossroads and another crossroads south east of Escoville.

- The 6th Airborne Brigade of General Kindersley reinforced the area held by the paratroopers.

- The 1st Special Brigade of Lord Lovat - who was wounded on June 13th and then replaced by General Mills Roberts - protected the northern flank from Amfréville to Sallenelles. But it could not retain the Battery of Merville which would be finally silenced on August 17th.

In the morning of June 7th the R.U.R. captured Longueval, while the "Devons" were taking Hérouvillette which was to be used later as a starting base for the "Ox and Bucks". The latter pushed on to Escoville which was heavily defended by the grenadiers of the 21st *Panzer*. The front line was brought to Hérouvillette-Escoville where, the Scots of the 51st Division (Highland) took over on June the 12th facing Ste Honorine which would be taken a month later.

On **June 8th**, a counter-attack of the 346th German Inf.Div. set out from Bréville across the fields where the gliders had landed and tried to recapture Hauger. Commandos and paratroopers were deadly accurate. 360 German

*Above: June 11, 1944. Major General Gale who commanded the 6th Airborne Division in front of his HQ at Ranville with the flag of the British airborne troops in the background. Opposite: a tank of the 13/18 Hussars supporting the airborne troops (I.W.M. photos)*

casualties were left on the northern slope. The men of General Gale had exploited the situation well. His principle was that as a seaman makes use of the wind and tide, so must an infantry commander make use of the terrain.

In the South east, between Hérouvillette and the bridges, the orchards, gardens and hamlets surrounded by high stone walls made defence easy enough. The Germans were to realise this on June 6th and 7th. They did not try to launch new assaults.They thought it enough to pepper the area with artillery and mortar fire. In the south from Longueval to Escoville stretches a bare plateau. Here one could see the wrecks of armoured vehicles abandoned by the 21st *Panzer*. In the east the main German bastion was the village of Bréville. It was the place where all their counterattack against the bridges would start.

During the night of **June 12-13** after a bombardment by the artillery of the Division supported by that of the 1st Army Corps, 2 battalions of the Parachute Rgt. and 2 battalions of commandos, plus an armoured squadron were hastily launched against Bréville which was finally cleared by midday.

It was a costly battle for the 6th Airborne and the Blackwatch of the 51st Scottish Division. It was the turning point of the fighting at the bridgehead on the

*Above: some men of the 12th Parachute Battalion taking a cup of tea on June 10. Opposite: Captain B. Priday (Centre) and two paratroopers of the "Ox and Bucks Light Infantry" at Hérouvillette on June 15 (I.W.M.)*

River Orne. After such terrible confrontations there would follow merely routine patrol actions and the daily discomfort of mortar fire, rain, and mud.

On **June 16** the 4th Commando Brigade of Brigadier Leicester came to reinforce the line at Bretteville-la-Côte. The position would remain as it was for a month during which time these highly trained men expected to receive orders to leave this sector for another mission where their skills could be put to better use.

The signal for an advance eastwards was actually given on **August 17**. Meanwhile the capricious Normandy summer saw repeated spectacular actions and audacious attacks and also austere days of observation and defence with the constant harrassment of the mortars, Stalin Organs and artillery in the daytime and of the Luftwaffe nearly every night, while the anti-aircraft guns displayed fantastic fireworks. During the month of June the losses of the 6th Airborne amounted to 215 officers and 2750 men - that is 1/5 of the complement with similar losses for the commandos and the 51st Scottish Division. On July 14 General Montgomery and General Gale came to Bréville to observe the plain towards the south. The bridgehead of the Airborne Division was to be used as a base for the first great offensive of British Armour east of Caen on July 18. Operation "Goodwood" would

14

*In Bois de Bavent. Opposite page: a patrol of the 5/7th "Gordon Highlanders" looking for German snipers advances cautiously (I.W.M. Photos). Above: Two German grenadiers of the 21st Panzerdivision, armed with a MG 42 machine gun, expecting a British assault. (Heimdal Coll.)*

not have the success which was expected. As the area held by the Parachute Rgt. grew, the 49th Division of General E. Barker took up position between the 6th and 51st Divisions on July 20. The 3rd Division was now facing Troarn.

In August the parachutists were still containing the Germans in the north east of the front where the main engagements were taking place. They received reinforcements: the Belgian motorised Brigade (Colonel Piron) and the Dutch Brigade (Princess Irene) for operation "Paddle" - the offensive towards the River Seine on a line starting from the coast to the road Caen-Paris. The 3rd Parachute Brigade captured Putot-en-Auge on **August 19**, then Dozulé while the 5th Parachute Brigade entered burning Pont-l'Evêque on **August 22**.

On the **27th of August** General Gale received the orders he had been awaiting for so long. He was to withdraw his troops from the front line and get ready for new missions more suited to paratroops. At that time the division was holding a line Pont Audemer-Honfleur. In the course of this action, the first great airborne operation in history, the 6th Division had suffered 4457 casualties including 821 men killed in action.

**Visiting the battlefield.**
Those who died in fighting are buried in the War Cemetery of **Ranville** together

Above: A paratrooper mounting guard in front of the HQ of the 6th Airborne (author's coll). Opposite: Chester Wilmott, a BBC war correspondant talking to French commandos (IWM). Below: At Thaon tanks of the 4th British Armd. Brigade driving to the front. (PAC)

with commandos, airmen, and soldiers of the Services and also some German soldiers: all those warriors being united for ever in Norman land. 2238 graves are in charge of the War Graves Commission in this cemetery near "Vieux Moulin" where one can see a memorial tablet commemorating the Belgian Brigade. Near by is the crossroads of Ranville and the memorial of the 13th Battalion of the Parachute Regiment which captured the village.

At **Hauger** stands a memorial to the Commandos.

At **Amfréville** one can see a memorial plaque of the 1st Commando Brigade.

At the **Battery of Merville** which so often changed hands between June 6 and August 16 a memorial has recently been set up in commemoration of the 9th Battalion of the Parachute Regt. (Col. Otway and his comrades in arms).

At **Le Mesnil** a monument recalls the struggles of the 1st Canadian Parachute Battalion to keep control of the impor-

*Above: At Thaon, The 4th British Armd. brigade driving to the front (PAC). Opposite: on the top of the page: a 155mm gun of American origin used by a Canadian Artillery Regiment (Author's coll). Bottom: A British 5.5 in. heavy gun at Creully (IWM).*

tant crossroads. The buildings of the pottery sheltered an advanced field hospital while divisional mortars were stationed in a quarry near by.

Then go to **Bénouville** over Pegasus Bridge. On the left one can notice the markings showing the exact position of the gliders of Major Howard for the raid the night of June 6. On the other side of the bridge stands the first liberated house in France - a pub - which is always a rallying-place for British veterans just as it was in 1944. A **museum** was opened by the Comité du Débarquement in 1974 in memory of the paratroopers and commandos who established and maintained the bridgehead on the River Orne.

# A.2. The installation of the 2nd British Army in its bridgehead and the Canadian front in the west of Caen from June 7 to July 8 1944.

In the British sector the battle for the beaches was won and finished by mid-day on June 6 at the cost of 2500 casualties. By the evening of D-day 3 assault Divisions had practically reached their objectives.

From east to west let us consider the 3rd British Infantry Division of General Rennie, the 3rd Canadian Infantry Division of General Keller and the 50th British Infantry Division of General Graham. During the first fortnight of June those divisions established their base. It was easy enough due to the poor preparations of the Germans. The 3rd Brit.Inf. Div. established a firm link with the 6th Airborne in the east and provided it with logistic support. In the west the 50th Div. made contact with the 5th American Corps. The immediate aim of General Montgomery was to slow down the military operations until enough supplies and reinforcements had been stored up behind the front lines. This was a necessary precaution as German counter attacks could be foreseen. It was necessary to keep the initiative to build up forces unhindered behind the front line and at the same time to continue the offensive in order to gain good bases for future advances.

## 1) The 3rd British Inf.Div.

In the afternoon of June 6, the 8th brigade of the 3rd Inf.Div. had been first to encounter a Panzerdivision, the 21st

*Above: At Bayeux on June 7 at 9.30 a.m. amphibious tanks of the 8th Armd. brigade (photo Maurice). Opposite page: top. General Bradley (1st US Army), Montgomery (21st Army group), Dempsey (2nd British Army) meeting at Blaye Bottom: some infantry units of the 3rd Canadian Inf.Div. going past the grounds of Château de Cairon (PAC).*

21

*Above: Rockets being installed under the wings of a "Typhoon" at Fresne-Camilly at the end of June 1944 (IWM). Below: Some grenadiers of the 12th Panzerdivision walking through Bully towards the front line (Munin). Opposite page: Two "Regina Rifles" at Bretteville-l'Orgueilleuse on June 13 (PAC)*

Panzer. One of its tank battalion had driven towards the sea in the gap left between the British and the Canadians. The Germans received orders not to go on with their operations, so they retired in the evening abandoning some thirty smouldering wrecks between Periers and Mathieu. This was the one German counter-attack which actually reached the sea.

The first days were employed in clearing out the German strongholds. The job was done by 2 other brigades of the 3rd division at Colleville and at Douvres where a radar station was finally taken by the Scots with the help of Churchill flamethrower tanks after a week of stubborn resistance. Caen was the objective of the 3rd division for the evening of D-day or in the morning of the 7th. But it was unable to go further than the wood at Lebisey, 4 kilometres short of the town. This wood was to be the front line of the division facing the elite troops of the 12th SS-Panzerdivision and the 21st Panzerdivision.

---

**Places to visit.**

- The blockhouses of the **radar station** on leaving Douvres towards Basly and those of **Hillman point** on leaving Colleville in the south.

- The war cemeteries of **Douvres-la-Délivrande** (942 graves) and **Hermanville** (1007 graves). Some of the British soldiers who fell during a month of static warfare in the north of Caen. The cemetery at **Cambes-en-Plaine** contains some of the soldiers of the 59th (Staffordshire) division who fell on July 7 and 8 at Saint-Contest, Epron, in the northern suburb of the town which they could not enter.

- **At Creully**, the little château de Creullet was the HQ of General Montgomery (21st Army Group) until June 19. In the medieval castle of Creully a memorial plaque on a wall reminds the visitor that for 2 months radio programmes were broadcast from this place daily by the teams of BBC-Normandy.

- Visitors should look for signs of the war: walls which have collapsed or which were pierced by shellfire, some ruins. Many fences have been made out of the landing strips of 90 odd airfields which dotted the countryside.

## 2) The 3rd Canadian Division:

It reached the RN 13 (the road from Paris to Cherbourg) in the evening of the 6th, but its armoured reconnaissance group had to retire because it was not supported. Yet it was overlooking Carpiquet Airfield, its objective. In this assault division all soldiers were volunteers. It suffered badly at the hands of the armoured regiment and the grenadiers of the 12th *SS-Panzerdivision* ("Hitlerjugend") on the 7th and 8th of June at Buron and Authie. The latter threatened

*Above: the town of Bretteville-l'Orgueilleuse after the German counter attack of June 8. The HQ of the "Regina Rifles" was destroyed; Opposite page, top: The fire control post of Canadian Artillery (PAC); bottom: a briefing of the "1st Canadian Scottish" in a farm at Putot-en-Bessin about June 15 (Author's Coll)*

the Canadian outposts at Bretteville-l'Orgueilleuse on the 8th. This counter attack was absorbed by the "Regina Rifles", the "Winnipeg" and the "Régiment de la Chaudière".

At Putot-en-Bessin the "Canadian Scottish" prevented the Waffen SS from crossing the Paris Cherbourg railway. After the disaster of the 27th Canadian armoured regiment (1st Hussars) at Mesnil-Patry on June 11 and the clearing of La Mue de Lasson at Rots the Canadian frontline in the north west of Caen remained practically unchanged until the beginning of July. On both sides there the men dug trenches, which grew stronger and stronger and less

uncomfortable. It was a static warfare which ended on **July 4th** with the assault towards Carpiquet airfield and the capture of Caen from the north west on July 9th.

That zone held by the Canadian division was the hottest of the front line during the first month of the campaign. Their opponents were fanatical Hitler Youth who fought with utter determination never to be seen again except possible at the very end of the war on German territory.

After the war the bodies of 13 Canadian prisoners who had been captured by this unit were discovered at the Abbey of Ardenne. They had been

*Above: A briefing of the "Highland Light Infantry of Canada" at Buron (PAC). Opposite page, top: "SDG of Canada" taking some grenadiers of the "HitlerJugend" prisoner in the north-western distric of Caen. Bottom: Two infantrymen of the "Règiment de la Chaudière" and their prisoners belonging to the 12th SS-"Hitlerjugend", 26th Rgt of grenadiers (PAC).*

assassinated - shot through the head. Later as an excuse for this war crime the Germans maintained that the Canadians had committed a similar blunder. Responsability for such a claim rests entirely with them - see "Grenadiere" by K.Meyer p. 230-231, the assertion is confirmed by General Eberbach. This shows how far violence had gone in June in the north west of Caen.

### Places to visit:

**At Villons-les-Buissons** some streets have been named after the Canadian units which stayed for a month in the village. At Château des Buissons - nicknamed "Hell's Corner" by the Scot-

*Above: 2 men of the "Durham Light Infantry" (DLI) at Tilly-sur-Seulles on June 15 (IWM). Opposite page, top: A group of Canadian officers at Putot-en-Bessin (Author's Coll); bottom: some men of the military police of the 3rd Canadian Inf.Div. at Bretteville-l'Orgueilleuse (PAC).*

tish Canadians or "Glengarrians", 2 plaques have been set up on the walls and on a monument along the road.

At **Buron**, on the main square stands a monument to the glory of the Highland Light Infantry of Canada who suffered heavy losses in the liberation of the village and of the men of the Sherbrooke Fusiliers.

At **Rozel** one can see the 1st example of the gratitude of local population to their liberators on the local war memorial.

At **Rots**: 2 plaques commemorating n°46 Commando of the Royal Marines who fought in the valley of the River Mue.

At **St Germain-la-Blanche-Herbe/ Authie** one can admire the Abbey of Ardenne where the 12th *SS-Panzerdivision* had established their headquarters.

The Canadian soldiers who fell in the fierce engagements are buried in the war cemetery of **Beny-sur-Mer** (2047 graves).

### 3) The 50th Division (Northumbrian)

It joined the 3rd Canadian Infantry Division on June 7 in the evening at Brouay in the east. It was the one unit of the 2nd Army to reach its objectives. Some patrols of the 56th Independent brigade entered Bayeux in the evening of June 6. There they encountered but a few Germans not too eager to fight. The British soldiers spent the night at St Sulpice and in the morning of June 7 tanks and infantry poured into the town while tricolors were brought out by cheering crowds after 4 years in hiding. On **June 12th** General de Gaulle paid a visit to this small sous-préfecture - possibly the only town of Normandy left intact. Bayeux was then the new capital of liberated France and also a leisure centre behind the lines for allied soldiers.

On **June 8th** Port-en-Bessin had been cleared after 2 days of fighting by n°47 *Royal Marines* which had joined up with the 29th US Infantry Division on that very evening. It meant that the gap between the 1st US Army and the 2nd British Army had been closed.

The 50th Inf.Div. and its neighbour, the 7th Armoured Division "the Desert Rats" had both fought in the Lybian desert. It had to get used to a rather peculiar terrain between Tilly and Villers-Bocage, very different from what they

*At Douet-de-Chouain on June 11. Above: "A" Company of the DLI of the 50th Inf. Div. and tanks going to the front line at Tilly. Opposite page, top & bottom: some Sherman tanks of the 79th Armd. Brigade on their way to encounter the "Panzer- Lehr" at Tilly-sur-Seulles (IWM).*

had seen in Africa. It would stay in this area for nearly a month during which both men and machines became worn out.

It was a sector easy for the Germans to defend. The German *Panzer-Lehr* (the third German armoured division on the British front) was the most powerful armoured unit on the German side in Western Europe. It possessed 2800 vehicles including 180 modern tanks. However, it had lost some of its vehicles on the way to the front because of allied air attacks. In 3 weeks the fighting around Tilly was to dismantle it.

### Places to discover.

This sector is dotted with war cemeteries. The most important one is situated in **Bayeux** where 4142 soldiers of the Commonwealth lie in peace. There is also an impressive War memorial to commemorate those reported missing (1837).

100 metres from that resting place a museum was installed in 1981 to commemorate the Battle of Normandy. There one can follow the events from June 7th to August 22nd 1944. It is open everyday from March to September and at the week-end the rest of the year.

In the Cathedral of Bayeux a plaque commemorates the 56th Brigade which liberated the town. One can also see the badge of the 50th Infantry Division painted on a wall in rue des Bouchers. In front of the south gate of the cathedral there is a plaque to the 50th Inf.Div.

The cemeteries of **Brouay** (377 graves) and of **Ryes** (652 graves) contains many soldiers of the 50th British Inf.Div.

*At Tilly-sur-Seulles. Above and opposite page, top: After the capture of the town on June 19, clearing mines (IWN), opposite page, bottom: This was Tilly ! nothing is left.*

Opposite page, top: another picture of Tilly showing clearly that the town was nearly completely destroyed. (Author's Coll.). Above and opposite page, bottom: Cristot on June 17 after the 49th Inf. Div. had cleared the place. The church is in ruins and so is the farm in front of the church. (IWM).

At **Ducy-Sainte-Marguerite** a monument was erected to the "Tyneside-Scottish" of the 49th division which, like most units of the 2nd British Army was stationed around Bayeux.

One kilometre south of the crossroads of Douet-de-Chouin, along the Bayeux-Tilly one can see the smallest of the British war cemeteries. It is called **Jerusalem** – the name of a hamlet of the civil parish of Juaye-Mondaye. Here were buried 47 soldiers who died at the field hospital of Jerusalem – one among the numerous field hospitals which could be seen around Bayeux.

## A.3. The battle of Tilly or the attrition of the German front.
## 7 to 25 June 1944.

During the week which followed the capture of Bayeux the grass of the rich meadows disappeared, covered with huge heaps of stores of all sorts, dumps of equipement, repair shops, depots, field hospitals and landing strips. Security in the bridgeheads was almost complete, provided by thousands of antiaircrafts guns. The allied assault divisions progressed cautiously in those places where the Germans were collapsing under the assaults of the guns and of the aircrafts.

The front then stabilised in the whole zone of the 1st Army Corps. Only probing attacks were made towards Tilly and Villers-Bocage.

Le Douet du Chouin was reached on **June 8** by reconnaissance vehicles of the Army Corps, but they were unfortunately strafed by American fighter-bombers at that crossroads. This sort of mistake will be repeated nearly everyday during the battle of Normandy, so near were the armies to each other. On June 8 the villages between Bayeux and Tilly were conquered by the 50th British Infantry Division supported by the 8th armoured brigade. But the German resistance stiffered that very day when the German armoured division "Panzer Lehr" arrived on the front. It absorbed, reorganised and sent back to the front line the German troops of this sector who were really exhausted after the fighting of the first two days. All the British attacks broke against a solid wall of German armour till the beginning of July. In spite of the losses due to air attacks which it had suffered before even reaching the front - 5 tanks and a lot of vehicles - the "Panzer-Lehr" held a front of 7 kilometres with its 184 tanks and 600 armoured vehicles. From Fontenay-le-Pesnel to Hottot the struggle between the tanks of both sides was really unequal. The German tanks well-concealed were superior in armement and thickness of armour. These would open fire on the Shermans and Cromwells more than 1500 metres away. They would catch fire in rapid succession unable to fight back against the "Panthers" with any effect. Only the naval artillery and the Typhoon rockets of the RAF managed to stop the offensive of that German unit towards Bayeux.

*Opposite page and above: On June 14 near Lingèvres, the 1st aid post of the DLI (50th Brit. Inf. Div.) with both German and British casualties. Below: at Livry, some soldiers of the "Rifle Brigade" of the 7th Armd. Div. and their prisoners of the 2nd Panzerdivision. (IWM).*

The German attack was stopped at Ellon on **June 9**. Later the German tank crews would take great pains to conceal their vehicles under branches transforming them into moving copses. Let the gleam of the sun on a piece of metal be seen by any allied airman or by an artillery observer, and in a matter of minutes a deluge of shells of all calibres would rain on the suspected vehicle and soon the naval guns of the battleships would open up and join in from 25 kilometres away. The "Tiger" or "Panther" tanks of 45 or 60 tons were blown skywards like bits of straw under the impact of the shells which soon turned the peaceful meadows into a lunar landscape with craters 5 metres deep. Tilly will remain the objective until **June 18**. The soldiers of the 56th brigade conquered the ruins of this village which had been crushed under the fire of allied artillery and German mortars. Engagements with tanks

*Above: near Colleville-Cheux, some soldiers of the 11th British Armd. Div. with their prisoners. Opposite page, top: At Fontenay-le-Pesnel, the counter attack of the 12th SS-Armd Regt. (Heimdal coll.). Bottom: in Le Haut-du-Bosq at Cheux, the Scots of the "Royal Scots" and some grenadiers of the SS-"Hitlerjugend" who were captured after the british offensive. (IWM).*

would go until the **beginning of July**; at Lingèvres and in the plain of Fontenay English tanks were knocked out at the rate of 3 to 1. In this war of attrition the Allies would have the last word for the Germans had no reserves available whereas the British had constant reinforcements at their disposal.

Meanwhile the 7th Armoured Division of General Erskine launched a daring attempt to outflank the front at Tilly on June 12. But it met a new *Panzerdivision* at Villers-Bocage. It was the 2nd *Panzer*, formed at Wien in Austria and a SS battalion of "Tiger" tanks (*SS Pz.Abt.101*). This assault of the "Desert Rats" was stopped dead in that town;

their armour had to turn back and take a defensive position at Livry until the month of July.

There had been two reasons for this failure: two armoured divisions arriving together on the same objective without enough preparation and the superiority of German equipment added to the greater experience of the German tankmen. The "Tiger" tanks appeared on the front at Villers-Bocage for the first time. The Allies imagined them to be similar to the 45 ton "Panther" they had been able to destroy in the Canadian sector on June 8. Even old "Model IV" with a 75 m.m. gun had been taken for "Tiger" tanks, commanded by the German ace, Michael Wittmann, broke up the spear head of the 7th Arm.Div. (the 22nd arm.Brigade) by surprise on **June 13**. The smoking wrecks of 27 British tanks and numerous vehicles were left on the spot. For that reason Villers-Bocage remained in German hands for 2 months and the 7th Arm.Div. with its light and medium tanks would be used for more specific uses e.g. quick exploitation of the terrain.

East of Tilly, the 49th Inf.Div. (West Riding) had taken Cristot on **June 13** and was now fighting on the line St Pierre/Les-Hauts-Vents/Fontenay-le-Pesnel, supported by some tanks against the *SS-Panzergrenadiere* of the "Hitlerjugend" supported by the antitank defenses of the "Panzer Lehr" in the west. The violence of the engagements around Fontenay could be compared with what was happening in the Canadian sector 5 kilometres in the west. At Château d'Audrieu English and Canadian prisoners were assassinated, while grenadiers and tankmen of the "Panzer Lehr" suffered the same fate. For that reason the 49th English Inf.Div. was knicknamed the "murderous bears" by the Germans. One must remember that the badge of the division pictured a polar bear since the 49th div. had been formed in Iceland. The plain south of Fontenay would be the centre on the fighting until mid-July.

June 26. "Epsom". The assault towards Grainville-sur-Odon: the 6th "Kosb" of the 15th Scottish Inf. Div. Opposite page: the 12th section of "B" company in an orchard. Above and below: the assault is protected by a smoke screen. (IWM).

*June 26, "Epsom", The Odon Battle. Above: a hedge - ideal cover for this rifleman of the 15th Scottish Inf. Div. ready to open fire. Opposite page: men of the 6th "Royal-Scots-Fusiliers" advancing through in Saint-Manvieu (IWM).*

## Places to discover.

- **Tilly-sur-Seulles**: The British War cemetery (990 English graves and 234 German graves) and the Museum of the Battle of Tilly in Chapelle du Val.

- **Hottot**: The British cemetery (1005 graves) and the monument in memory of the soldiers of the 231st Brigade of the 50th Inf.Div. and of the Dorset Rgt. in front of the town-hall.

- **Fontenay-le-Pesnel**: The memorial of the 49th Inf.Div. and the British cemetery (460 graves) along the road to Granville. The civil parish has close links with the members of the Hallams-Club, in memory of the Hallamshire battalion (York and Lancaster) which finally captured this German bastion on June 25-26.

- **Villers-Bocage**: a street has been named after the 4th County of London Yeomanry (armoured) which was badly mauled by the 13 tanks of Wittmann on June 13.

On June 22 the losses in the British sector amounted to 29,156 killed wounded and missing.

# A.4. The Battle of Odon: Operation Epson. June 25 to July 10.

It was the first large scale offensive, the objective of which was the plain south of Caen after crossing the rivers Odon and Orne from the departure line Cristot to Norrey-en-Bessin. The 8th and 12th Corps were in charge of this operation, supported by the 49th Inf.Div. of the 30th Corps at Fontenay. After preparation by the 600 guns of the Army Corps, supported by the heavies of the navy, the 15th Scottish Division was in Saint Manvieu by midday, the 11th Armoured Division reached Cheux followed by the 43rd Inf.Div. (Wessex) assisted by 3 armoured brigades. Facing them the division "Hitlerjugend" though badly mauled was holding its ground.

The spear head however powerful was getting more and more blunt as the offensive met villages in chaos under accurate hits of German antitank guns and the harrassment of snipers. On **June 26** a bridge on the River Odon was captured intact at Tourmeauville by the "Argyll and Sutherland Highlanders" which defended it until the arrival of the tanks. This bridge would be the favourite target of German gunners for weeks and they could not destroy it. The 11th Arm.Div. swept over the bridge after losing some tanks on the northern slope of Hill 112. So strong was the antitank defense from that high place that the Shermans had to drive back to Baron which was being cleared by the Scots. At the same time other battalions of the 15th Scottish Inf.Div. had taken another bridge on the River Odon and at Gavrus where they consolidated a small bridgehead foreseeing an inevitable German counterattack.

June 28, the Odon Battle ("Epsom"). Opposite: the crews of Bren-carriers and a M-10 of the 49th Inf. Div. resting near Rauray (IWM). Above: At Rauray, two men of the DLI examining a "Tiger" tank of the 101th heavy SS-Battalion (IWM) and the same place today. (E.Lefèvre/Heimdal).

It took place the following day and was carried out by the SS 2nd Armoured Corps which had just arrived on the front and which regrouped the 9th and 10th *SS-Panzerdivision* ("Hohenstaufen" and "Frundsberg") equipped with "Panther" tanks, self-propelled guns and "Mark IV"s. The 10th had not got its "Panther" Battalion. The encounter took place from Gavrus to Cheux which was reached by the "Panzer", but they could not take this village thanks to the furious British antitank defence. The assault was renewed on **June 28th** but the 8th British Corps kept its positions except on Hill 112 at the foot of which the Battle of Odon would rage for a month. Fontaine-Etoupefour was stormed by the British in the beginning of July. Verson was threatened by the 43rd Inf.Div.

which failed at Maltot on **July 10th** facing units of the 2nd SS-Armoured Corps (1st company of the 102th SS-battalion of heavy tanks). For a month all these units, except the 11th Armd.Div. would stay at the foot of hill 112, near the River Odon, harrassed by the "Nebelwerfer"-rockets - which made up for the lack of field artillery, and also by showers of mortar shells. The "Tigers" and "Panthers" always patrolled the area and launched deadly counter-attacks against the heavy "Churchill" tanks of the armoured brigades and the Scottish, Welsh (53rd Inf.Div.) soldiers or those of the Wessex.

The climax of this battle can be placed on July 10th. It was Operation Jupiter carried out by 2 brigades of the 43rd British Inf.Div. and the Shermans of the 4th Armoured Brigade. The battalion which was leading the assault directly towards the summit of Hill 112 was decimated soon after passing the cross, 400 metres from the wood topping the hill. This unit, 800 men, the 5th battalion of the Duke of Cornwall (5th D.C.E.I.) was wiped out by a charge of the "Tigers". It was to be withdrawn and placed in reserve.

At the same time the battalions of the Hampshire and Dorset Regiments were decimated as they were progressing towards Maltot through the corn fields. They had started from the Château de Fontaine-Etoupefour. Maltot itself was a village which had been heavily fortified by the Waffen-SS. Such attempts also failed at Eterville and Esquay-Notre-Dame where the Germans dominated the plain which did not offer any possible shelter for English attackers. More than 7,000 men fell in a few days. The objective: a breakthrough to the River Orne

*At Rauray, June 28 and 29. Opposite page: an SS sniper being taken away by two British soldiers walking in front of the "Tiger" tank pictured on page 45 (IWM) and the same place now. (Lefèvre/Heimdal). Above: a column of Sherman tanks of the 24th Lancers of the 8th Brit. Armd. Brigade driving past a German "Panther" which was destroyed while defending this strategic sector (IWM). Bottom: the same place as it is now. Some bits of the shed can be seen in the grass.*

the crossing of the river and the surrounding of Caen from the south was not attained. But those encounters managed to hold and engage more and more German forces and armour round Caen to allow a breakthrough and a rupture of German resistance in the American Sector where at that time there were only a hundred German tanks.

### Places to discover.

- **Secqueville-en-Bessin**, the British Cemetery: marshalling zone for Epsom.

- **Saint-Manvieu**, the British Cemetery (1627 graves). The names of some streets commemorate the liberation of the village by the "Royal Scots Fusiliers" and their comrades in arms of the 15th Scottish Div.

- **Tourville**, names of streets are a reminder of the "Scottish Corridor". The monument to the 15th Scottish Division stands between Tourville and the bridge of River Odon captured by the "Argyll" (Moulin de Taillebosq).

*Opposite page: At Secqueville-en-Bessin on July 1, British artillery pounding the front line with 5.5 guns. Above: at Lingèvres on June 20, The wrecks of 2 "Panther" tanks of the Panzer-Lehr. Below: the machine gun battalion of the 43rd Inf. Div. (Wessex) crossing the river Odon. (IWM).*

*Above: June 28, the 29th Armd Brigade of the 11th Armd Div. getting ready to attack at Baron-sur-Odon. Below: a battalion of machine guns of the 15th Scottish Inf. Div. using the railway as a road during their advance towards Grainville-sur-Odon and Noyers-Bocage (IWM).*

*Above: near Hill 112, the church of Evrecy. The picture was taken at the end of June before the end of the fighting (Heimdal coll.). Below: near Hill 112 after the war. This is like the scene at Verdun in 1918 (Lerond/Heimdal coll.).*

*Above: on the top of Hill 112. This Sherman tank of the 4th Armd. Div. swung round when its track caught in the trunk of a tree. The wreck was used by German spotters. This picture was taken after the war (Lerond/Heimdal coll.). Below: The town of Caen burning: this is a German picture taken from the railway station (Bundesarchiv).*

*At Caen on June 27. Monsieur Guerrier (his name meant warrior !) who was in charge of supplying the Bon Sauveur hospital with food. He is seen here driving his cart in front of Saint-Pierre church.*

*Above: July 9, Caen in ruins; Saint-Pierre church has lost its spire. Below: July 9, in the evening: the French flag being hoisted in front of the Abbaye aux Hommes in Caen (IWM).*

*Carpiquet aerodrome. The Canadians had to fight hard to conquer the place which was held by some young soldiers of the "Hitlerjugend" (Author's coll.).*

## A.5. Operation Charnwood. 4 to 9 July 1944 : The Capture of Caen.

While of offensive of the beginning of July was developing around Hill 112 and in the plain of Eterville at Maltot, the 3rd Canadian Inf.Div. had progressed towards Carpiquet which defended Caen from the west with its antitank defenses.

The fighting which followed brought the Régiment de la Chaudière and the "Queen's Own Rifles" to the village of Carpiquet on **July 6**. But the nearby airfield was cleared after 4 days of fighting against a company of SS-Grenadiers of the "Baby Division", the "Hitlerjugend", supported by some tanks buried up to the turret. The rockets of the Typhoons destroyed those bastions and the Canadians had to use their flame-throwers against the last casemates held by teenagers.

- **Baron**, a street bears the name of the Scots. At the Château a plaque commemorates General Mac Intosh Walker who was killed there. **Hill 112** also called hill of Calvary by the Germans because of the granite cross which still stands there. Near by is the monument to the 43rd Division along the road Caen to Aunay-sur-Odon. At 800 metres on the left, at the crossroads of the road to Condé, stands a monument to the Dorset and Hampshire.

The capture of Caen. Above: the "Warwicks" of the 59th Brit. Inf. Div. advancing towards Caen. One can see the church of Saint-Contest (IWM). Below: Saint-Jean church a strong medieval building which withstood the devastating bombing unlike more modern buildings (R. Dalasalle).

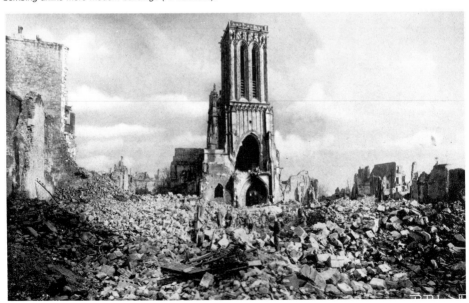

*Caen. Saint-Pierre church seen from the Rue de geole the street is blocked by debris. The spire was hit by 406 shell from the battleship HMS Rodney (Author's coll.).*

Caen. Above: Saint-Pierre square (IWM). Below: The area around Saint-Jean church was totally destroyed. In this moonlike landscape only a few bits of wall were left standing. As the British historian Henry Maule says it was a picture of the "end of the world" that the Tommies found when they entered Caen. Civilian losses amounted to 6000 men, women and children. Was such bombing really necessary when the front line was outside the town ? (PAC). Opposite page, top: Saint-Pierre square in front of the ruins of the Hôtel d'Escoville. An armoured vehicle of the 17th Duke of York's RCH, a reconnaissance unit of the 3rd Canadian Inf. Div. which entered Caen on July 9. Bottom: A Canadian artillery observation tank entering Caen. (PAC).

During the **night of July 8 to 9** a last carpet of 2500 tons of bombs was dropped on the northern districts of Caen : it was the 1020th air raid warning of the war. The 3rd Inf.Div. and the 59th Inf.Div. advanced towards the fortified hamlets in the northern outskirts of the town while the 3rd Canadian Inf.Div. was taking Franqueville and the Abbey of Ardenne, holding Carpiquet firmly despite the fire of the "Nebelwerfer". The British were considerably impeded by the confusion created by the bombing and the resistance of the men of the 16th division of the Luftwaffe (infantry). At 13h30 after rearguard action, the Germans abandoned the norther half of Caen and crossed over the River Orne which divides the town into two parts at that very moment. The "Stormont Dundas and Glengarry Highlanders of the 9th Canadian brigade were first to reach the centre of Caen. The 3rd British Inf.Div. and the 3rd Canadian Inf.Div.

*Opposite page, top: The Place des Petites Boucheries. The arrival of tanks of the 1st Hussars of the 3rd Canadian Inf. Div. in the Rue du général Moulin. Above: Gunners of the 1st KOSB with a 6 pounder anti-tank gun in Rue du Vaugueux looking to Abbaye aux Dames on July 9. (IWM).*

*Caen, July 10. Above. Sergeant Goddard of the Army Film Photo unit (AFPU) is seen filming what is left of the Hôtel Moderne - a surrealistic sight ! (IWM). Opposite page, top: a local woman pointing to the site of her house while talking to a British dispatch rider. (IWM). Bottom: the right bank of the River Orne. Some lorries of the Army Service Corps driving towards the front now at May-sur-Orne (Author's coll.).*

met in the Place Saint-Pierre. They received a tremendous welcome from the local population who had lived through the trials of the battle.

10,000 Tommies had died in the battle for Caen which had been the objective of the 3rd Inf.Div. for D-day. 3000 civilians had also died under the ruins of their houses and in the streets. On **July 10th** the losses of the 2nd British Army had reached 22,208 casualties.

## Monuments:

- At the north west of Caen, District of Chemin-Vert, stands the monument of the "Glengarians", the first unit to enter Caen in the morning of July 9.

At the western entry of Caen (direction of Bayeux) stands the monument of the "Regine Rifle Regiment" which was quartered in Caen for a while and forged friendly links with the local Resistance Movement (Fred Scamaroni company) who was often used as guides. A commemorating plaque has been set up at the crossroad of Pont de Vaucelles and Quai Meslin.

- Place Monseigneur des Hameaux, there is a plaque commemorating the liberation of the town of July 9 at the spot where the French flag bearing the Lorraine Cross was hoisted in front of Abbaye aux Hommes where 10,000 people had found a refuge during the battle.

- Boulevard Bertrand a plaque recalls the name of the first Canadian soldier killed in the town: gunner Hill. It is placed on the wall of the gardens of Préfecture.

- Rue de la Délivrande a moving cross above the town symbolises the suffering of the civilian population and the liberation (Calvaire Saint-Pierre).

- 2 civilian monuments must be noted. One in the Cemetery St Gabriel, the other one at Chapelle St Georges in the castle of Caen where are deposited the ashes of one of the victims of the bombings of July 8-9.

## A.6. Operation Goodwood: The failure in the attempt to break through east of Caen towards Falaise : July 18-29 1944. The Canadian operations Atlantic and Spring: 18-25 July.

In the morning of **July 18th** 700 British tanks drove south from the bridgehead of the Airborne troops on the River Orne after a fantastic air bombing with 7000 tons of fragmentation bombs which did not form craters. The idea was to leave the ground intact for armoured vehicles to roll through. The terrain, the plain to the east of Caen was ideal for armour :

*Operation "Goodwood". Above and opposite page: Infantrymen of the 3rd Inf. Div. are carried on the tanks of the 13/18 Hussars near Ranville (IWM).*

Wide open fields, no hedges : only farm buildings with thick walls and scattered hamlets which proved excellent antitank defenses for the Germans.

The aim of the operation, besides the destruction of German material and the elimination of their troops, was mostly the continuation of Montgomery's plan i.e. to force the enemy to play the part assigned in his plan. This offensive threatened a breakthrough in the plain to the south and east of Caen, thereby opening the road to the River Seine and Paris. The Germans expected this attack and Montgomery did his best to make them believe it was his intention. To oppose this the Germans had fortified the villages surrounding Caen. They had buried tanks and as many forts manned by squads of grenadiers equipped with antitank weapons. The *SS-Panzerdivisionen* : 1st ("Leibstandarte Adolf Hitler"), the 9th ("Hohenstauffen") and what was left of the 12th ("Hitlerjugend")

*Above: Three grenadiers of the 26th regt. of the 12th SS Div. caught in their foxhole during the assault of the 15th Scottish Div. around Grainville-sur-Odon on June 29. (Author's coll.). Below: After "Epsom" on June 28. A German 105mm howitzer abandoned after the battle. (IWM).*

*Above: Villers-Bocage being bombed by a Lancaster of the RAF on June 15 (IWM). Below: The memorial placed on top of Hill 112 in July 1944 by the 5th DCLI of the 43rd Inf. Div. after the deadly assault of July 10 and 11. (Author's coll.).*

*Above: July 18, to support "Goodwood" a Canadian 4.2 mortar firing at a factory at Colombelles (Author's coll.). Below: near Caen a PzKpfw IV of the 1st or 2nd SS Armd Corps (Landrieu/Heimdal coll.).*

*Above: July 20. A British Sherman having problems while negociating a bend in the narrow streets of Hérouvillette east of the River Orne (IWM). Below: Some Canadian Fusiliers of Mont Royal at May-sur-Orne on July 28 (PAC).*

supported by the 21st and 2nd *Panzerdivisionen*, the 272nd Inf.Div. and the 3rd Flak Corps were used on the east and south front of Caen. 6 out of the 8 German armoured divisions were always stationed in the Caen area and only the "Panzer Lehr" and the 2nd *SS-Panzerdivision* ("Das Reich") had joined the front near Saint Lô.

The 8th and 1st British Army Corps progressed well enough in the beginning. The 11th Armoured Division and the Armoured Division of the Guards was leading while the 7th Armd.Div. was ready to exploit any advantage. The 3rd Inf.Div. supported by the 27th armoured brigade was driving towards Troarn.

The Shermans burst into flames in rapid succession 1500 metres north of RN 13 in the west of Cagny. The 88mm guns of the Flak (German Antiaircraft Defence) scored direct hits on the leading squadrons of the 29th brigade of the 11th Arm.Div.

In a matter of minutes some 40 Shermans caught fire. The armoured columns which followed them bypassed them on the right and drove towards the heights of Bourguebùs beyond the railway Paris-Caen. The combats continued for 2 days in front of the villages : Bras, Hubert-Folie, Bourguebus, Soliers. 400 British armoured vehicles were destroyed (of which 250 could not be repaired) with the gain of only 6 kilometres east of Caen allowing the widening and the deepening of the zone in which British armour could lick their wounds.

On the right flank of Goodwood, on **July 18**, the 3rd Canadian Inf.Div. backed up by the 2nd Canadian armoured brigade had cleared the right bank of the River Orne and all the villages, then the steel mill at Colombelles and Mondeville. At the same time some elements of the 8th brigade were crossing the Orne in Caen and had joined the rest of the division at Vaucelles at nightfall

*May-sur-Orne, July 28. Above: an armoured vehicle of the Royal Engineers of the 2nd Canadian Inf. Div. driving past the church. Opposite page: some fusiliers of Mont Royal and a tank of the "Fort Garry Horse" which has been destroyed (PAC).*

of July 18th. Operation Atlantic was a success: all its objectives were reached including the villages of Louvigny and Fleury-sur-Orne in the south west of Caen which fell into the hands of the 2nd Canadian Inf.Div. on July 18-19. It was the first time it was seriously engaged. From **July 20** the front stabilised south of Caen.

The 2nd Canadian Inf.Div. between the River Orne and the road to Falaise supported by the Canadian tanks and the Cromwells of the 7th Armd.Div. was now facing the 2nd and 116th *Panzerdivisionen* and the 9th *SS-Panzerdivision*. On the other side of RN 158, the Canadians of the 3rd Inf.Div. and the infantry of the 11th Armd.Div. near Bourguebus were facing the 1st *SS-Panzerdivision*("LAH") at Tilly-la-Campagne which would fall only on August 8.

An operation of harrassment was mounted for July 25th. Its code name was "Spring". The purpose was the capture of May-sur-Orne, Rocquancourt and Tilly-la-Campagne. It was also to maintain pressure on that part of the front to fix German armour at the moment when the Americans were launching their breakthrough west of Saint-Lô. On **July 23** the 1st Canadian Army of General Crerar took command of the area. Operation Spring was its first engagement. This diversion was particularly costly for the Canadians at May-sur-Orne, and Tilly-la-Campagne and round the farms of Beauvoir and Torteval.

By July 19th the losses of the 2nd Army were 34,700 killed wounded or missing. The Canadians suffered 2900 casualties between July 18 an 30.

## Places and monuments.

- There is no monument to "Operation Goodwood". - **Louvigny**: Monument to the "Royal Regiment of Canada", the Fort Garry Horse (armour of the 2nd brigade) and the 4th RCA (Canadian Artillery).

- **Saint-André-sur-Orne**: Monument to the "Blackwatch Regiment of Canada" which used this village as a

72

Opposite page: At Evrecy, near Hill 112, end of July, Welsh soldiers driving Norman cows (IWM). The breakthrough in the Bocage ("Bluecoat"). Above: At St Martin-des-Besaces on July 30, protected by a tank of the 23rd Hussars (11th Armd. Div.) some elements of the 8th "Rifle-Brigade" are crossing the road from Villers-Bocage to Vire at a place called La Ferrière-Haran. Below: At Cahagnes on July 31st, some men of the 7th Armd. Div. clearing the verges of mines. (IWM).

departure base towards May-sur-Orne and to "Regiment de Maisonneuve" which cleared the banks of the River Orne from Fleury to Saint-André.

- **May-sur-Orne**: on the local war memorial there is a plaque commemorating the "Regiment des Fusiliers Mont-Royal".

The victims of the fighting of the end of July can be found in the British cemetery of Banneville-la-Campagne (2170 graves) and the Canadian cemetery of Bretteville-sur-Laize (2957 graves including 2790 Canadians).

# A.7. Operation Bluecoat: The offensive of the 2nd British Army in the bocage country of Vire. July 31st - August 7th.

This purely British operation was entrusted to the 2nd Army of General Dempsey. It was scheduled to relieve the American armies who were deeply engaged driving south on the western flank. The battlefield was the bocage area of Caumont, Bény-Bocage and Vire. No valuable German forces had been detected in this sector since they were concentrated in the south and in the east of Caen.

This operation started on **July 31** from Caumont towards Saint-Martin-des-Besaces which was reached on August 1st, towards Bény-Bocage reached on the 3rd and towards Presle captured on the 4th. Villers-Bocage on the eastern flank was taken on August 4, Aunay-sur-Odon on the 5th and the 30th Corps reached the Hills of Normandy, the highest summit being Mont Pinçon (329 metres). The siege of Mont Pinçon lasted 3 days. At the beginning the 8th Corps became entangled in jams on the departure line: too many vehicles and too many people on narrow roads. It met two lines of hills 8 kilometres further south, those of Estry and Pierres. Such natural obstacles were judiciously used by the German reinforcements (21st *Panzerdivision* and 9th *SS-Panzerdivision*) which just as they had done in Tilly in June had the advantage of their superior armement. For a week there lasted

*Opposite page : the 15th Scottish Inf. Div. is advancing south of Caumont on July 31st. Above: At Cahagnes on August 2, a tank driving past a stray horse near a damaged petrol pump. The sign points to the HQ of machine gun battalion of the 7th Armd. Div. Below: "Bluecoat". A Honey tank followed by Shermans of the Coldstream Guards on August 2 in the sector of Bény-Bocage. (IWM).*

*Above, top: "Bluecoat", some elements of the Guards Armd. Div. south of Saint-Martin-des-Besaces on August 2. Above, bottom: The "Warwickshires" of the 3rd Brit. inf. Div. near Carville on August 2. A dispatch rider and the tractor of a 6 pounder anti tank gun. Opposite page, top: Near Ondefontaine on August 4, the 43rd Inf. Div. facing German resistance. Opposite page, bottom: a Bren-Carrier in Monchauvet on August 6. (IWM).*

*"Bluecoat". Above: near Mont-Pinçon on August 7, Sergeant Clifford Brown of the Somerset Light Infantry quenching his thirst during a pause between engagements. Opposite page, top: On August 8 near Mont-Pinçon, a squad of infantrymen of the 43rd Inf. Div. in an anti-tank position on the crest of Bas-Perriers. Opposite page, bottom: On August 10, British infantrymen looking for snipers. One of them is wearing a German army belt as a trophy. (IWM).*

tank fighting at Bas-Pierre, Chênedollé and Estry. A hundred tanks of the 11th Arm.Div. and the Armoured Division of the Guards were knocked out. The 8th Army Corps suffered 2000 casualties. Then the 30th Corps drove towards Condé-sur-Noireau the "soft belly" of German front.

Meanwhile Evrecy and Hill 112 had been finally cleared by **August 12** by the 12th corps and a new bridgehead on the River Orne was created at Thury-Harcourt by the 59 British Inf.Div. The result of this offensive was a gain of 25 kilometres across the bocage, from Caumont (July 31) to Thury-Harcourt (Aug.8), Condé-sur-Noireau (Aug.14) and Flers (Aug.15). This relieved the American push in the west. It also prevented the German counter-attack towards Avranches on August 7 from mustering enough armour, for this could

not be withdrawn, from "Bluecoat" sector where a mobile system of defence had been made necessary by the characteristics of the terrain.

**Places and monuments:**

The War cemetery at **Saint-Charles-de-Percy** (744 graves).

The plaque set up at **Thury-Harcourt** to commemorate the 59th Inf.Div. (Staffordshire).

At **Flers** the memorial to the 11th Armd.Division.

78

# A.8. The push of the 1st Canadian Army towards Falaise. Operation Totalize and Tractable. August 7 to August 16 1944.

For a week the British and the Canadians launched minor probing operations against the villages fortified by the Germans in the west and south of Caen. These pinned down the main bulk of the German 7th Army in Normandy. The offensive towards Falaise started on **August 7** at 23 hours. After 3500 tons of bombs had been dropped 4 armoured columns rushed forward on either side of the main road Caen-Falaise. They

consisted of 400 tanks, the armoured vehicles of the Engineers and infantry carried on special armoured transport vehicles (Kangaroos). They were driving due south and they were guided by the tracer shells of the light guns of the antiaircraft defence, by projectors lighting the clouds to create a sort of artificial moonlight and many other clever devices. The frontal attack was defended by only the 89th Inf.Div. and the remnants of the 12th *SS-Panzerdivision* supported by the 88mm guns of the 3rd Flak Corps used as antitank weapons. Actually a German counterattack was to stem the American flood spreading out from Avranches by a special order of Hitler. To do so Marshall von Kluge had been forced to muster all possible *Panzerdivisionen* including

80

those which were trying to contain the allied pressure at Caen and to replace them by infantry units. The result was that the 2nd and 3rd Canadian Inf.Div. and the 51st Scottish Inf.Div. and their support of 2 armoured brigades backed up by the 720 guns of the 1st Army did not meet with insuperable difficulties in seizing their first objectives. The second phase of "Totalize" began on **August 8** at midday. Two brand new divisions were to drive through the positions conquered the night before. They were the 4th Canadian Armd.Div. (General Kitching) and the 1st Polish Armd.Div. (General Maczeck).

A bombing raid by the 8th American Airforce dropped 1500 tons of bombs which fell partly on the assembly area causing 310 casualties. Among these was General Keller who was wounded and had to abandon command of the 3rd Canadian Inf.Div. 4 kilometres were gained by the 2 armoured divisions which met the "Tiger" tanks of the 101st battalion of heavy tanks SS belonging to the 12th *SS-Panzerdivision* at Cintheaux. On August 9 a whole Canadian armoured regiment (the 28th, British Columbia) was decimated on Hills 140 and 111 near Estrées-la-Campagne by the 12th SS reduced to the strength of a regiment (essentially "Kampfgruppe Waldmüller" and "Kampfgruppe Krause", some tanks of the 12th with the "Tiger" tanks of the 101st all under the command of Colonel Wünsche, a little artillery south of the River Laizon

*Above: The 1st Polish Armd. Div. at Grainville-Langannerie on August 5. Opposite page: The 4th Canadian Armd. Div. at Cormelles-le-Royal before operation "Totalize" (PAC).*

and some elements regrouped from the remnant of the 89th Inf.Div.).

On **August 11th** "Operation Totalize" came to an end in front of strong wall of antitank defences of determined Germans though very inferior in number. The front was now half way between Caen and Falaise. The Allies had lost 5500 men and they had not managed to reach Falaise as scheduled.

**Operation Tractable.**

On **August 14** at noon unending columns of Canadians armour were progressing east of the RN 158 through ripening cornfields under a blazing sun. 3700 tons of bombs had been dropped.

Unfortunetely tragic errors were made once again causing 400 victims among the 2nd Canadian Corps. This Corps included the 700 tanks of the 1st Polish Armd. Division, the 4th Canadian Armd.Div. and 3 more armoured brigades. It dismantled the lines of the 89th and 85th German Infantry Divisions.

On **August 15** Potigny was cleared by the 1st Polish Armd.Div. It is worth noting that this village was inhabited by miners of Polish extraction. Meanwhile the 3rd Canadian Inf.Div. was clearing Montboint Olendon and reached Soulangy only 5 kilometres from Falaise. Here and there could be seen some

"Tiger" tanks lurking behind a hedge or antitank guns crouching behind a crumbling wall. But this was only the delaying actions of the rear guard of the 1st SS-Corps which had regrouped the remnants of the 12th SS-Panzerdivision ("HJ"), the 89th, 85th and 271st Inf.Div. and was trying to keep open the jaws which were closing between Argentan and Falaise while the 7th and 5th German armies were retreating eastwards in good order.

At the date of August 13th, the 12th *SS-Panzerdivision* which once was a crack and powerful division was left with the following elements:

- 20 tanks, including the "Panzerjäger": self-propelled tank-destroyers, 1 section of grenadiers on armoured vehicles, 300 grenadiers, a reconnaissance team, 1 battery of 88mm Flak with 4 guns, 1 battery of 37mm Flak with 9 self propelled guns, 1 company of 20mm Flak, 3 batteries SFH, 1 battery of 100mm guns. 20 tanks against hundreds: after two months of hard fighting the German army had been completely worn out by the Battle of Normandy, even before reaching the Falaise Pocket.

On **August 16** the 4th Canadian Armd.Div. and the 1st Polish Armd.Div. were now going in the direction of Trun, towards the south east. The Poles crossed the River Dives at Jort and the Canadian armour at Morteaux-Coulibeuf.

The 2nd Canadian Inf.Div. received the proud mission of taking Falaise a most coveted objective since the failure of Operation "Goodwood" on July 18th.

On **August 17** the "Camerons" and the "South Saskatchewans" entered Falaise supported by a squadron of tanks of the "Sherbrooke Fusiliers". But it was the job of the "Fusiliers de Mont-Royal" to clear the town. 60 young grenadiers of the "HitlerJugend" were entrenched in the local highschool. At 02h00 on **August the 8th** the "Fusiliers du Mont-Royal" liquidated this bastion which was the symbol of resistance to the bitter end. The 60 young people preferred dying together instead of obeying an order to retreat. A German air attack hit both friends and foes. There were only 2 "Tiger" tanks to cover the retreat of the last elements of the 12th SS at Nécy: they would be soon destroyed.

Then the 1st Canadian Army and the 2nd British Army began their irresistible advance towards Trun and Argentan, pushing before them 100,000 Germans in full flight. They had to be trapped between Trun and Chambois, and they were at Saint-Lambert-sur-Dives and Coudehard on August 21st.

On **August 24th** the Forces of the Commonwealth and those attached had suffered 82,309 casualties including 11,000 for the Canadians.

**Places and Monuments.**

- The war cemetery of **Bretteville-sur-Laize** already mentioned: 2790 Canadians graves.
- The Polish war cemetery of **Langannerie**: 650 graves of the soldiers of the 1st Polish Armoured Division.
- On **Hill 111**, between Estrée-la-Campagne and Maizières, stands a monument to the 4th Canadian Armd.Div. whose 28th armoured regiment was destroyed in this place and on the neighbouring Hill 140.

- At **Fontaine-le-Pin**, the church possesses stained glass windows commemorating the sacrifice of the Canadians of the 1st Army.
- At **Jort**, a plaque commemorates the crossing of the River Dives and of River Laizon by the Polish tanks on August 15-16.

---

*After battle in the British sector the Norman countryside is dotted with graves. Opposite page, top: A Sherman tank by the side of the grave of a grenadier of the 12th SS-Panzerdivision (IWM). Opposite page, bottom: A Cromwell tank of the 7th British Armd. Div. destroyed during operation "Goodwood-Atlantic" on the crest of Verrières, south of Caen. In the foreground the grave of private Smalley (Author's coll.)*

*The tomb of a British Officer in the military cemetery of Bayeux.*

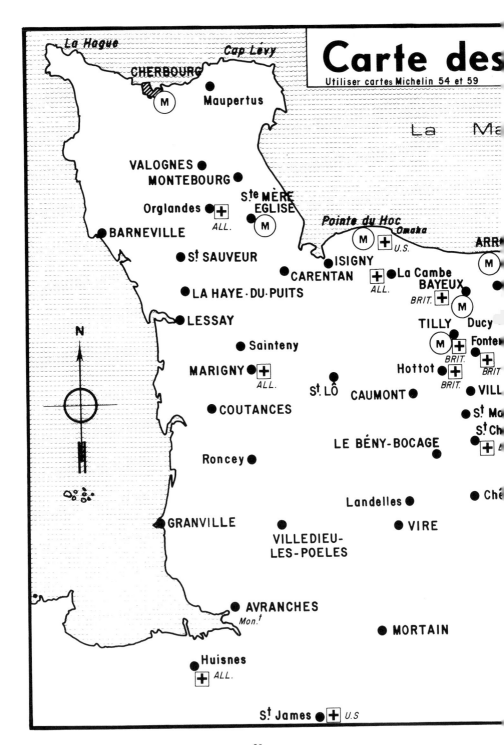

La Hague · Cap Lévy

# Carte des

Utiliser cartes Michelin 54 et 59

La Manche

CHERBOURG ● Ⓜ Maupertus

VALOGNES ●
MONTEBOURG ●

Orglandes ●✚
ALL.

S.te MÈRE EGLISE Ⓜ

Pointe du Hoc · Omaha

Ⓜ ✚
U.S.

BARNEVILLE ●

ARR●

Ⓜ

S.t SAUVEUR ●

● ISIGNY

● CARENTAN

✚ ● La Cambe
ALL. BAYEUX

● LA HAYE·DU·PUITS

BRIT. ✚ Ⓜ Ducy

● LESSAY

TILLY

Ⓜ ✚ Fonte●
BRIT. ✚
BRIT.

● Sainteny

Hottot ● ✚
BRIT.

MARIGNY ●✚
ALL.

St. LÔ ●

CAUMONT ●

● VILL

● COUTANCES

● S.t Ma

St Ch
●
✚ ●

LE BÉNY·BOCAGE ●

Roncey ●

● Ché

Landelles ●

GRANVILLE ◄

●
VILLEDIEU·
LES·POELES

● VIRE

● AVRANCHES
Mon.t

● MORTAIN

Huisnes ●
✚ ALL.

S.t James ● ✚ U.S

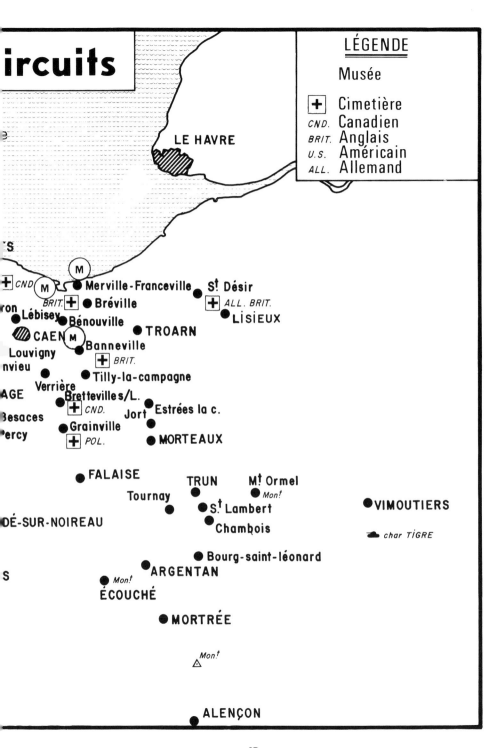

**ircuits**

LÉGENDE

Musée

| | |
|---|---|
| ➕ | Cimetière |
| *CND.* | Canadien |
| *BRIT.* | Anglais |
| *U.S.* | Américain |
| *ALL.* | Allemand |

LE HAVRE

'S

➕ *CND* Ⓜ️

Ⓜ️

● Merville-Franceville ● S⁺ Désir

*BRIT.* ➕ ● Bréville ➕ *ALL. BRIT.*

ron ● Lébisey ● Bénouville ● LISIEUX

💠 CAEN Ⓜ️ ● Banneville

Louvigny ➕ *BRIT.*

nvieu ●

● Tilly-la-campagne

Verrière

AGE ● Bretteville s/L.

➕ *CND.*

Besaces Jort ● Estrées la c.

Percy ● Grainville

➕ *POL.* ● MORTEAUX

● FALAISE

TRUN M⁺ Ormel

Tournay ● ● *Mon⁺*

● S⁺ Lambert

DÉ-SUR-NOIREAU ● ● VIMOUTIERS

● Chambois

🡆 char TIGRE

● Bourg-saint-léonard

S ● ARGENTAN

● *Mon⁺*

ÉCOUCHÉ

● MORTRÉE

△ *Mon⁺*

● ALENÇON

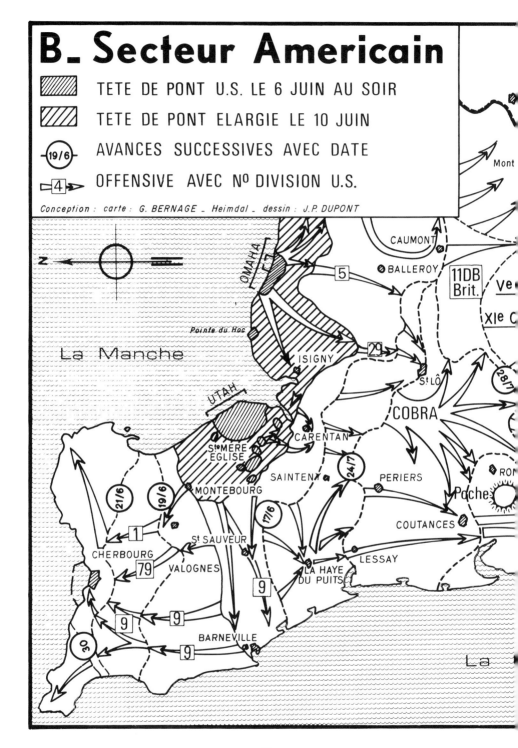

# B_ Secteur Americain

TETE DE PONT U.S. LE 6 JUIN AU SOIR

TETE DE PONT ELARGIE LE 10 JUIN

AVANCES SUCCESSIVES AVEC DATE

OFFENSIVE AVEC N° DIVISION U.S.

*Conception : carte : G. BERNAGE _ Heimdal _ dessin : J.P. DUPONT*

CAUMONT

OMAHA

BALLEROY

11DB Brit.

Ve

Mont

5

XIe C

Pointe du Hoc

La Manche

ISIGNY

29

St LÔ

28/7

UTAH

COBRA

CARENTAN

St MERE EGLISE

SAINTENY

24/7

PERIERS

ROM

Poche

MONTEBOURG

17/6

21/6

19/6

1

COUTANCES

St SAUVEUR

LESSAY

CHERBOURG

79

VALOGNES

LA HAYE DU PUITS

9

9

9

30

BARNEVILLE

9

La

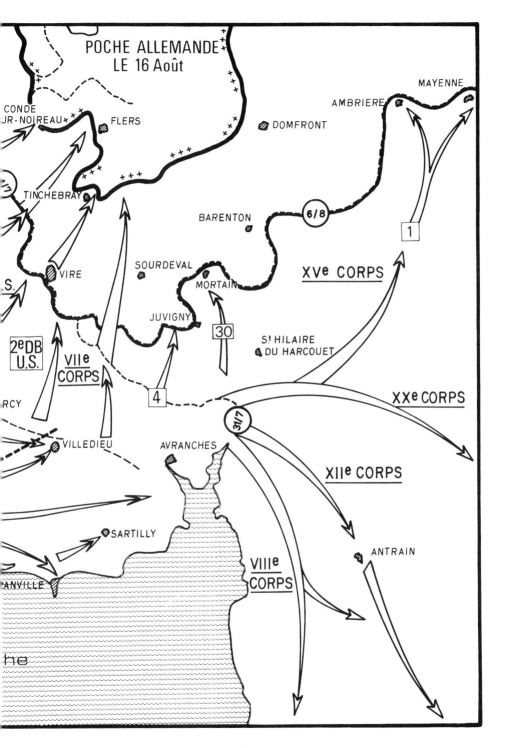

POCHE ALLEMANDE
LE 16 Août

MAYENNE

AMBRIERE

CONDE
SUR-NOIREAU

FLERS

DOMFRONT

TINCHEBRAY

6/8

1

BARENTON

VIRE

SOURDEVAL

XVe CORPS

S.

MORTAIN

JUVIGNY

30

St HILAIRE
DU HARCOUET

2e DB
U.S.

VIIe
CORPS

4

XXe CORPS

RCY

XIIe CORPS

VILLEDIEU

AVRANCHES

SARTILLY

ANTRAIN

VIIIe
CORPS

ANVILLE

he

# B. THE AMERICAN SECTOR

The American battlefield is less dotted with monuments, war cemeteries or vestiges than the English sector. Traditionally American commemorative ceremonies take place in the war cemetery of Saint-Laurent/Omaha beach and at Sainte-Mère-Eglise/Utah beach. Most American monuments can be found in these places. Yet the American breakthrough and progress in Normandy has been by "Voie de la Liberté" - Liberty Highway starting from Sainte-Mère-Eglise and Saint-Lô. It takes tourists to Rennes and Nantes. Special milestones always well kept are a reminder of this sweeping drive south.

The American sector originally began on the landing beaches on June 6 at Omaha-Beach (Saint-Laurent/Vierville) and Utah-Beach/Sainte-Mère-Eglise.

The two original American bridgeheads were linked later on when Carentan was captured on June 12. Then they spread out in the east as far as Caumont and included Cotentin on June 26. It would take a whole month for the American sector to reach the road Lessay/Saint-Lô.

---

*Below: An M.P. of the 1st US Army directing traffic at the bridge over the River Douve at the north western entry Carentan on June 15. Opposite page, top: At Saint Côme-du-Mont a paratrooper of the 101st Airborne Div. and his German prisoner. The latter is wearing a French military belt whereas the American has collected a German bayonet and hand grenades - June 10. Bottom of the page: Medals are given by General Bradley to Colonel Vandervoorte of the 82nd Airborne Div. and to other soldiers who were the heroes of the 1st day (US Army photos).*

*Above: At Carentan on June 12. A German prisoner being driven away on the front of a jeep of the 101st Airborne Div. Opposite page, top: some GIs of the 4th Inf. Div. walking through Sainte Marie-du-Mont. Bottom: At Orglandes on June 9th. German prisoners being interrogated by an intelligence squad of the 82nd Airborne.*

at the cost of 70,000 casualties. After the breakthrough, the crossing of Coutances and the capture of Avranches on July 30, the American army would fan out in Brittany, stretch to Le Mans on August 10, reach the River Seine on August 19 and Paris on August 25. Out of over a million GI's who had landed on the Normandy beaches, the Americans suffered 124,394 casualties.

## B.1. The installation of the 1st US Army in the airborne bridgehead in Cotentin peninsula: June 7 to June 16 1944.

### B.1.1. From Omaha-Beach.

By midday on June 7 the 29th and 1st

*Opposite page: At Neuilly-la-Forêt on June 9 some infantrymen of the 29th Inf. Div. talking to the local "curé". Above: At Sainte Marguerite-d'Elle on June 16, a GI in his foxhole reading "Stars and Stripes" while another one is reading a letter frome home. (US Army photos).*

USDIV had finished clearing the beach at Omaha, at the cost of 2,200 casualties. A German counter attack was repelled near the church of Vierville that very morning. But the regular fighting of a German 105mm battery caused more casualties during the day and made the situation there rather uncomfortable.

The 2nd US Inf.Division landed at Saint-Laurent in the afternoon of June 7 and the 3 divisions of the 5th Corps of General Gerow began their war in the Norman countryside: They captured La Cambe where they destroyed a German antitank position and Formigny at the end of the day. Those two villages marked the farthest advance of the American units at midnight of June 7.

Other hamlets fell into American hands on the outskirts of Omaha on June 8. At Pointe du Hoc the last German fighters had been eliminated by the 2nd Batallion of US Rangers which had then been reinforced by the 116th Inf.Rgt of the 29th US Inf.Div. This put an end to the heroic historic assault on the beach on June 6. Infantry units supported by tanks and tank-destroyers were attacking everywhere. A junction was made with the 30th British Corps at Port-en-Bessin. Colombières was reached thanks to a pontoon-bridge built by US engineers across the flooded valley of the River Aure. All the objectives set for the 5th Corps for the 6th of June had been reached by June 9th, except the small town of Trévières which fell the following day.

The deepest advance towards the east was made in the Forest of Cerisy Where the 2nd US Inf.Div. captured Balleroy, while the 29th US Inf.Div. was progressing from Isigny towards Carentan.

On the German side, after the first clashes, General Marcks who was in command of the 84th Corps reshuffled his troops after getting reinforcements from Brittany. The 3rd German parachute Division of General Schimpf and the 353th German Inf.Div. of General Mahlmann came to back up the 352nd Inf.Div. which had had to yield ground on June 6th but still kept 60% of its efficiency. Teams of Engineers of the 84th Corps were preparing positions of defence to protect Saint-Lô. These were based on the terrain which they had to keep and defend at all cost: the bocage, which was a mosaic of fields surrounded with banks covered with hedgerows, bushes and trees.

The plan of the operations of the 5th Corps according to the orders of the 1st US Army of General Bradley was to have Caumont taken by the 1st US

*Above: Carentan, June 14. It was the first Norman town captured by the American troops. Opposite page, top: At Montebourg on June 21. An armoured car of a reconnaissance unit of the 1st US Army entering the town. Bottom: Montebourg was destroyed by air attacks, field artillery and naval guns. (US Army photos).*

Inf.Div. (General Huebner), Bérigny and Hill 192 east of Saint-Lô by the 2nd Inf.Div. and Saint-Clair-sur-Elle/Couvains by the 29th Inf.Div. on June 12 and 13. These objectives were achieved according to schedule with the exception of Hill 192 which was only taken at the beginning of July after fierce fighting against the paratroopers of the 3rd Division. The 5th US Corps had not yet encountered German tanks apart from a few self-propelled antitank or assault guns. Later General Gerow will be able to write that the 1st US Inf.Div. was the only one to have met a Panzerdivision at Caumont. This 2nd Pz.Div. had been formed at Vienna in Austria. The Americans managed to make it swerve from its original axis. Four German armoured divisions were opposed to the British troops in the neighbouring sector at the same moment. The plan of General Montgomery was to pin down as many Germans as possible in the British sector to make it easier for the 1st American Army to take Cherbourg (7th Corps starting from Utah) and then break through towards Brittany.

But by mid June the only horizon enjoyed by GIs who were fighting from Saint-Jean-de-Daye to Bérigny and Caumont was the next hedgerow, a farmhouse a few yards ahead transformed into a bastion or a big elmtree a few yards ahead. All these were the target of artillery of both sides for days. It was the war of the hedgerows at Graignes, La Meauffe, Villiers-Fossard, Bérigny. The advance of the 5th Corps, now supported on the left by the 19th Corps of General Corlett was stopped 5 kilometres north of Saint-Lô "as if the bridgehead was not to go farther". The fantastic American war machine had got entangled in the Norman bocage. The superiority of the GIs in machines and

technology was useless. From now on it was only men with their rifles that counted. General Bradley said that to vainquish German resistance and the Bocage nothing but Infantry could be used. Nobody had found another means to get through. Besides towards **June 17** priority was given to the 7th Corps which was carrying out its assault on Cherbourg. Ammunition got even more scarce at Saint-Lô after the storm on June 19 which destroyed the artificial harbour of Omaha-Beach.

**B.1.2. The fighting to enlarge the bridgehead at Utah-Beach and the zone of the airborne troops.**

In the morning of June 7 the airborne troops of the 82nd and 101st Abn.Div. had conquered a zone of 30 square miles of lowlands from the Germans who were still resisting fiercely in numerous pockets in which they had entrenched themselves. Out of the 14,000 men who had been dropped in the first hours of July 6 only 6,000 had managed to form fighting units of some importance, while 6,000 could be considered as casualties and 2,000 were lost in the countryside and had to organise themselves as best as they could. In the morning of June 7 the 4th US Inf.Div. had joined with the paratroopers starting from a security zone 5 kilometres in front of Utah-Beach. The landing there had been reasonably easy as the GIs of those units had suffered "only" 197 casualties. Advancing on the narrow causeway across the flooded land behind the beaches, the units of the 7th Corps could capture companies of German soldiers cut off by the paratroopers. A strong link was established at Sainte-Mère-Eglise with the troops that had just landed, principally those of the four battalions of tanks. The 709th German

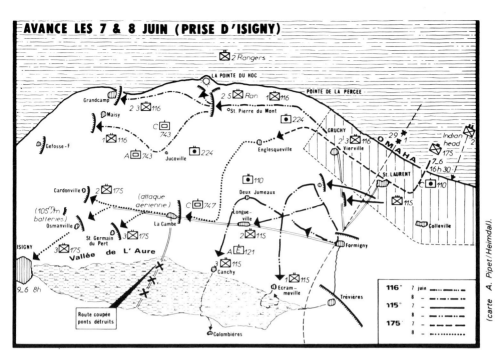

## AVANCE LES 7 & 8 JUIN (PRISE D'ISIGNY)

Inf.Div. was to lose 700 men, half of them coming from the 795th battalion of volunteers from Georgia (U.S.S.R.), during the fighting around Sainte-Mère-Eglise. In the meantime several battalions of the 82nd Airborne were having a tough time west of River Merderet where German counterattacks were kept in check at the cost of heavy casualties and wounded soldiers could not be evacuated during the fighting.

In the north the 4th US Inf.Div. (General Barton) tried to capture the coastal batteries of Azeville and Saint-Marcouf (Crisbecq). But these were concrete fortifications well organized and the 4th division bypassed them for the time being.

The 101th Arb.Div. of General Taylor positioned exactly between Omaha and Utah was to achieve the junction between the two bridgeheads. After driving off a counterattack by German paratroopers of the 6th Regiment (von der Heydte) who were trying to break southwards through the American line on June 7, the 101th Airborne firmly held the flood-gate at La Barquette and the bridges of the Port overlooking Carentan. This couterattack cost the German 100 losses and 400 prisoners. On **June 8** Saint-Côme-du-Mont was taken and troops began to regroup facing Carentan. Further east the 29th Inf.Div. was at Isigny and was getting ready to advance towards Carentan along the RN 13 (trunk road). Spirits were very high among the columns of infantry following the tanks: it was partly due to the fast advance from Omaha.

On the other side, in the north west of Carentan, on the same RN 13 the paratroopers of the 101th Abn. had four bridges to cross before they could reach the outskirts of Carentan. The road was 5 metres wide and on both sides spread flodded fields and the marshes of the Lower-Douve, the River Douve and le Merderet.

99

and charged the German paratroopers with hand grenades and bayonets at the cost of 480 casualties after two days of fightings. The 506th regiment took the place of the 502nd which was exhausted. The main attack was conducted from the northern part of the town on **June 12**. The battalions of the 327th/401st Rgt brought in by gliders had crossed the Lower-Douve north of Carentan which they had bypassed and were entering the town from the east at the same time. The day before at midday the infantry of the glider regiments had met elements of the 29th Inf.Div. at Auville-sur-le-Vey achieving the link between the 7th and the 5th Corps. One might have expected a powerful counterattack by German armour towards the sea between the two American bridgeheads aiming at dividing the American forces. It came 24 hours too late on **June 13** following the road from Périers to Carentan. It was mounted by the 17th SS-Panzer-Grenadier-Division "Götz von Berlichingen", a division of motorised infantry supported by a battalion of 37 assault guns and also by the paratroopers of the 6th Regiment (Colonel von der Heydte). The 17th SS-Pz.Gren.Div. (General Ostendorff) reached the southern houses of Carentan while the German paratroopers were fighting against their opposite numbers near the railway station. The American paratroopers suffered badly and were expelled from some of their positions in the south west of Carentan (Hill 30) by the SS assault guns coming from Baupte. But the 2nd US Inf.Div. rushed from Omaha with motorised artillery and the P.47 of the 9th American Air Force. Very soon things improved in Carentan and south of the town. The German onrush had been stopped and it had cost them 500 SS grenadiers and paratroopers.

*Opposite page: French civilians waving at Americans near Montebourg. Bottom: American engineers clearing Valognes of rubble. In the background one can see the ruins of Saint-Malo church. Above: The assault of Cherbourg is under way. This tired GI is not pleased to have to dig in. (US Army photos).*

On **June 10**, the 3rd battalion of the 502nd Rgt stormed the Douve river bridges well supported by the artillery from Saint-Côme, but it met a dense fire of small arms when drawing near Carentan. The 1st battalion then passed through the 3rd bridge badly mauled

On **June 14** American positions in Carentan were strongly held and there existed a firm link between east and west.

On **June 15th** the 8th American Corps (General Middleton) took care of this sector and the 101st Airborne came under its command. Its mission was to protect the base of the peninsula of Cotentin and also to guard the southern flank of the 7th Corps of General Collins who was about to move towards Cherbourg according to the plan of Montgomery.

---

**Touring the area.**

From Bayeux it is easy to reach the American military cemetery of **Saint-Laurent-sur-Mer** (9386 graves). The American monuments of Omaha-Beach concern June 6 and are situated at Vierville and Pointe-du-Hoc with a museum opened in summer **Omaha-Jour J** at Vierville. At **Isigny** one can see a memorial light on the main square to commemorate the liberation of the town. **La Cambe** possesses a German military cemetery (21,160 graves). At **Carentan** a monument commemorating the liberation and a monument to the 101th Airborne Division. One can then go to **Sainte-Mère-Eglise**, where one can recall the parachute drops of the night of June 6 1944. In 1964 a museum of the American Airborne troops was established. This museum is a must. **Utah-Beach** does not form part of this pattern but its monuments must of course be visited. One must not forget that the 2nd French Armoured Division landed on that spot on August 1st 1944.

# B.2. The battle for Cotentin peninsula. The siege and capture of Cherbourg from 18 to 26 June 1944.

General Montgomery's order of June 18 reminded General Bradley that his immediate duty was to take Cherbourg. To do so he had to cut off the peninsula by pushing through Saint-Sauveur-le-Vicomte towards Barneville. This would prevent German reinforcements and supplies reaching Cherbourg. The 7th Corps of General Collins supported in the south by the 8th Corps of General Middleton could now move towards Cherbourg by the shortest way i.e. via Valognes. Cherbourg would be taken and the peninsula would be cleared of all its German defenders. At the end of his message General Montgomery mentioned that he expected Caen and Cherbourg to be captured by June 24.

On **June 18** the 4th US Inf.Div. had steadily pushed the Germans (709th, 243rd, 91st Inf.Div.) north of a line Montebourg/Azeville/Crisbecq losing 2,200 men in a single week. The 9th Inf.Div. (General Addy) had been assigned the task of liquidating the last German strongpoints along the coast. Quinéville fell on June 15 after exceptionally hard resistance. Two regiments supported by tank-destroyers eventually overcame the defences of Quinéville with the help of artillery and the Air Force which had to use napalm bombs. This brought an end to the threat against Utah-Beach, with the clear result that now 4500 tons could be unloaded on the beach instead of 1500 tons before June 15. With the destruction of the last coastal battery all the objectives assigned to the 7th Corps for D-day had finally been reached. It was now mustering in the bridgehead painfully conquered by the 82nd Airborne along the River Merderet (la Fière) and was getting ready to cut off the peninsula from the continent.

The 90th US Inf.Div. had already tried to push westwards several times following the causeway leaving the Merderet. But each time it had been driven back by comparatively small enemy forces suffering heavy casualties. It was the first engagement of this unit in the Second World War. Its 358th regiment reached Pont-l'Abbé on **June 12** starting from Chef-du-Pont. The only living creatures they could find there were a couple of rabbits, and one of them did not look very cheerful ! On **June 13** the 90th Inf.Div. received a new commander (General Landrum). The rolling terrain stretching between the Rivers Douve and Merderet was one of the worst of all the Norman Bocage. The main element was of course the hedgerows, the earthbanks generally 5ft high covered with a solid mass of bushes, brambles and creepers just as tall and with trees towering 15 ft above them. In some places there existed twin hedgerows

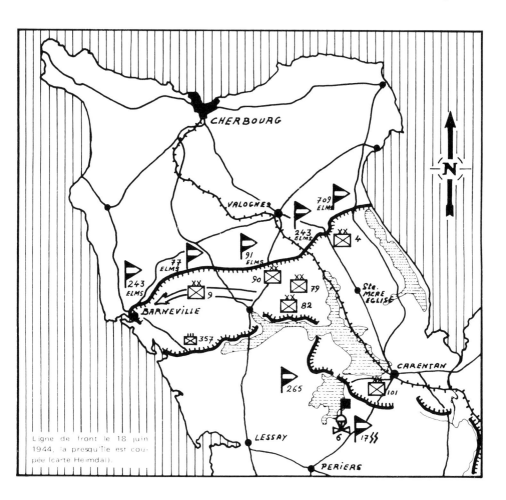

The investment of Cherbourg. Above: An American M 29 Weasel tractor of the 4th Inf. Div. carrying supplies in the north east of Cherbourg on June 24. Opposite page: A GI racing across dangerous crossroads leading to West-Cherbourg and La Hague. German resistance was concentrated around the naval dockyard which can be seen burning on June 27 (US Army photos).

separated by a drainage trench which made a perfect shelter. Each hedge could then form an excellent denfensive position thick enough and tall enough to give good shelter and good firing positions to the men of the infantry. The latter would make this wonderful situation more perfect by digging L shaped foxholes in the side of the bank and then perpendicularly. Those hedgerows separated the "clos" (meadows) turning each of them into as many tiny battlefields distinct from one another. It is easy to understand that tanks could not be used as taught at West-Point. Consequently the infantry companies had first to reach the next hedge before they could cross it. The crossing itself was a matter of using handgrenades and cold steel against an enemy using the same methods sometimes less than a couple of yards away.

One **June 15**, the 82nd Airborne was threatening Saint-Sauveur which was only 1 kilometre distant and which was still occupied by a regiment of the 265th German Inf.Div. just arrived from Brittany. The 90th US Inf.Div. was engaged in the east of Orglandes, the 4th was on its right and kept its pressure facing north. The 9th US Inf.Div. was progress-ing more easily westwards. It intercepted some elements of the 77th German Inf.Div. which was then reaching the front line. There were now 5 German infantry divisions in Cotentin. The Americans could oppose them with 5 infantry divisions all motorised and supported by tanks plus one Airborne Division. The Americans had superiority in number, equipement and quality with elite troops. In the **evening of June 16** the 82nd Airborne was holding Saint-Sauveur-le-Vicomte where the engineers spanned the River Douve allowing the tanks to exploit the gains: Sainte-Colombe was captured by the 9th US Inf.Div. which could not go farther than Néhou. Orglandes fell in the **morning of June 17** and the 9th US Inf.Div. entered Néhou which the Germans had evacuated during the night. Then this division advanced along the road going to Barneville-sur-Mer. They reached that place at the end of the day causing confusion among the Germans of the 77th Inf.Div. which was moving along the coastal road. The peninsula was cut off on the **18th of June**. The 9th, 79th and 4th Inf.Div. of the 7th US Corps took positions facing north (Cherbourg) while the 90th US Inf.Div. was occupying the transverse

zone which had been cleared from Barneville to Utah-Beach. On **June 19** after
a preliminary air bombing destined to
avoid street fighting Montebourg was
found to have been deserted by its German defenders. The 4th US Inf.Div. crossed it and the 9th US Inf.Div. entered
Bricquebec without any opposition
worth mentioning. On **June 20** at last
the 4th Div. entered Valognes which the
Germans had abandoned too. This fact
confirmed that the Germans were
regrouping in the defensive positions
around Cherbourg whose siege could
now begin. The German Commander in
Chief was General von Schlieben. He
had at his disposal all the troops gathered in North Cotentin i.e. about 40,000
men belonging to the 709th, 77th, 91st,

243rd Inf.Div. and a good number of
units belonging to the Navy, the coastal
artillery, Todt Organisation, Antiaircraft
defence (FLAK) and the assault battalion
AOK 7. The 3 American divisions met
with surprising aggression from the Germans 15 kilometres from Cherbourg.
This showed clearly that the Germans
had decided to resist for a long time in
good positions well stocked with food
and ammunition all around Cherbourg.
The landscape had also changed for the
GI's. The hedgerows were no longer
there. Instead there were meadows and
scattered woods in the highlands of
North Cotentin, with here and there
some granite boulders. On **June 21** the
Americans met the 2 main lines of
defence of "Festung Cherbourg". First a

*Opposite page, top: Artillery observers from various army and navy units with a good view overlooking Cherbourg
from "Pierre-Butée" on June 25. They are directing artillery fire on the defences and the Naval Dockyard. Opposite
page, bottom: The Château de Martinvast, south of Cherbourg on June 24 after its capture by the Americans. As it
stood near a V 1 launching pad it was also a target for allied bombers. Above: Infantry of the 79th Inf. Div. in the
Avenue de Paris in Cherbourg. They are seen here in front of the public gardens. (US Army photos).*

line running from Cap Lévi to Hardinvast, Martinvast, Sainte-Croix-Hague and Branville which resisted the probing attacks of the American assault companies supported by tanks as recommended by the soldier's hand book. The anti-tank guns well concealed, even half buried or in concrete casemates knocked out 36 Shermans on the 21st. The American Navy took position off Cherbourg to prevent any incoming supplies or a German retreat by sea. General Collins sent an ultimatum to General von Schlieben during the **night of June 21/22**. It was clearly shown that he was caught in a trap and that his situation was desperate. Nothing happened. As General Bradley could not afford a regular siege for it would have postposed the ultimate capitulation, an air attack on the main line of resistance was launched by 600 bombers on **June 22nd**. It was followed by another bombing raid made by 400 medium bombers which created considerable chaos in German communication lines and lowered the morale of the troops. The 4th US Inf.Div. starting from Maupertus on the 22nd captured the blockhouses and pill boxes one after the other until June 24. It had been backed by the 4th squadron of Cavalry which suffered a lot from the antiaircraft guns (FLAK) used as anti-tanks weapons.

The 79th US Inf.Div. (General Wynche) in the centre was being held in check at Hardinvast while the 9th Div. did not make much progress until June 24. For

*Opposite page, top: On the top of Fort du Roule on June 27. General Ira Wyche and Lieutenant-Colonel Gilman A.Huff with some men of their division, the 79th US Inf. Div. (US Army photo). Opposite page, bottom: Some US elements advancing towards the town centre after the capture of Octeville, rue Président Loubet. Above: The German garrison leaving Fort du Roule by the lower exit after its surrender (Photos Musée Lib. Cherbourg).*

days massive support was given by US artillery irrespective of available supplies in ammunition and also by squadrons of 12 fighter bombers of the US Airforce. Some results were at last obtained on **June 24**. The main German line of defence began to collapse at various points and many stongholds became isolated. A last ultimatum for unconditional surrender was sent by General Collins on the **25th** as 3 divisions were now fighting in Tourlaville, Fort-du-Roule, Octeville and Equeurdreville. In the meantime American heavy guns (155mm "Long Tom") were eliminating German concentrations and defences one after the other. The US Navy also played its part by attracting the fire of the German coastal batteries - particularly those in La Hague, which showed their positions to American observers. In no time fighter bombers equipped with rockets obtained spectacular results which spared both time and losses in the clearing up operations by the US infantry and artillery.

On **June 26** at last the lower storeys of Fort-du-Roule were neutralised. This caused the German commanders of the fortified town of Cherbourg, General von Schlieben and Admiral Hennecke to surrender with their complete staff to the 9th US Div. which sent them up to the 7th Corps.

*Above: After the fall of Cherbourg on June 27 and the capitulation of the last elements of the German defence, the GIs are patrolling the streets. In the foreground the bodies of four German soldiers. Opposite page: La Haye-du-Puits fell on July 8. Top, a squad of 81 mortars of the infantry of the 79th Inf. Div. and (bottom) German prisoners of the 9th Inf. Div. being marched towards Saint-Sauveur.*

But German resistance was to last longer. Commander Hermann Witt held on at the Naval Dockyard and an attack of the 47th US Inf.Rgt. of Colonel Smythe was necessary to deal with that stubborn resistance. It was launched at 8 o'clock a.m. on **June 27**. 2 hours later all resistance had ceased. Farther east in Val-de-Saire Major Kuppers was resisting in redoubt "Osteck" (south of Fermanville). He would surrender only on **June 28** at 8 a.m. In La Hague, west of Cherbourg, German resistance lasted even longer. The "Kampfgruppe Keil" ceased fighting at **midnight on June 30**. At daybreak of **July 1st** all German resistance had definitely come to an end in the northern part of the Cotentin peninsula. 10,000 prisoners had been captured in Cherbourg and 6,000 more had been caught by the 9th US Inf.Div. in La Hague during the fighting of the last days (June 27-30).

After fighting for 24 days in Cotentin the 7th US Corps had suffered 22,119 casualties (2,887 killed and 5,793 missing) among whom 4,660 were from the 82nd and the 101st Airborne Divisions. On the other side 39,000 German prisoners of war had passed through American camps in Cotentin before being ferried to Britain. The number of 14,000 German casualties (killed, wounded and missing) has been given for the same period in Cotentin.

At the end of June it was quite clear that the Germans had completely lost all hope of driving the Allied back to the sea. But the conquest of Cotentin did not break the German fighting power in Normandy for the time being. Hard fighting was to follow among the hedgerows until the end of July when the 84th and the 2nd German Corps tried to seal off the 1st Army in its bridgehead.

___

**Places to visit.**

- Go from Sainte-Mère-Eglise to **Cherbourg** via Montebourg and Valognes which were completely destroyed as one can see by the new buildings and houses which were rebuilt in the years 1950/60. A visit of Fort-du-Roule overlooking the town and the harbour of Cherbourg will allow you to understand why the Americans advance was but a series of jumps forward from one bastion to the next. The Museum of Fort-du-Roule (Musée de la Libération de Cherbourg) is worth visiting and befits the majesty of the place.

- **Barneville-sur-Mer**. At the exit of the town towards La-Haye-du-Puits a monument tells the visitor that the Cotentin Peninsula was sealed off in that place by the 7th Corps on June 18.

- The German military cemetery of **Orglandes** - between Valognes and Pont-L'Abbé is a place to meditate. 10,152 German soldiers lie in this cemetery.

___

# B.3. The hedgerow battle from La-Haye-du-Puits to Saint-Lô. June 27 to July 18 1944.

**B.3. The hedgerow battle.**

In his official report (M.505) of June 30 General Montgomery mentioned once more the main lines of his plan, so that all the commanders of the great allied units should never deviate from it.

*July 5. The 83rd US Inf. Div. while advancing of 600 metres in Saint-Eny (opposite page, top), captured 6 prisoners and lost 1,500 men. Opposite page, bottom: the capture of this young German prisoner - one of the 6 - cost the 83rd Div. on July 15 1500 losses (US Army photos).*

The hedgerow Battle. Above: A typical bocage landscape above the Saint-Lô/Périers road, where the powerful American war machine stuck. Below: an American 3 inches antitank gun opening fire during the slow advance towards Saint-Lô. Opposite page, top: each hedge had to be conquered separately. Bottom: US artillery observers forced to hide in the thick growth. (US Army photos).

His long term policy, once a bridgehead established firmly, had always been to attract the bulk of the German forces to the west flank (British sector) and to fight it there so that things might be easier on the west flank (the American sector).

This strategy had already paid dividends, since Cherbourg had been taken without the German High Command withdrawing a single one of their armoured divisions then fighting around Caen. The 1st American Army was now getting reorganised and was regrouping near Saint-Lô without any hinderance from the Germans. The plan was for the Americans to attack on July 3 with the 7th and 19th Corps in the centre while the 8 and 5th Corps would protect the wings. Once the breakthrough was achieved, the brand new 3rd Army of Patton would send the 8th Corps of Middleton along the western coast of Cotentin hastening south towards Avranches and Brittany and opening the way to the heart of France. Then this new army was to swing east towards the River Seine which should be reached at D+90. Whatever the German intentions might be no change in the initial plan would be accepted.

In the beginning of July 135,000 GIs were getting ready to attack La-Haye-du-Puits, Sainteny and Saint-Lô, starting from a departure line following the winding sunken lanes and hedgerows. The

*Above: At Saint-Clair-sur-Elle on July 4. Soldiers of the 2nd US Inf. Div. advancing with difficulty towards Hill 192. Opposite page: the 30th US Inf. Div. getting ready to cross the River Vire from Saint-Fromond. On July 9 (top) a light tank driving past a 90mm gun used as an anti tank gun. On July 10 (bottom of the page), some men of the US Signal Corps repairing the telephone lines while the infantry waits to advance. (US Army photos).*

*Opposite page: The River Vire was crossed at Saint-Fromond on July 7 by the 117th Inf. Reg. pushing towards Saint-Jean-de-Daye. The men of the 105th Engineer Combat Battalion had built a light bridge to allow the troops to pass. The bulk of the units would soon follow (see previous page) (US Army photos). In this sector the German paratroopers resisted doggedly. Some men of the 3rd German Parachute Inf. Div. (above) can be seen carrying a wounded comrade in the sector of Bérigny. Below: in the north of Saint-Lô, German paratroopers lying in ambush in the ruins of a farm. (Bundesarchiv).*

Americans had lost 18,374 men between June 6 and June 22. On July 11,000 more losses should be added reaching a total of 62,000 after the capture of St-Lô on July 18. At that date the total of the losses in the British sector which was bearing most of the German pressure was actually half that figure (34,000). The cause of such haemorrhage in the American army whose task should have been made easier seems to have been twofold: the lack of experience of the GIs in most of the divisions engaged in Normandy and also the excellent use made of the terrain by the Germans who were masters in the art of camouflage and ambush.

In the area north of Saint-Lô in early July the Hedgerows War was to acquire its full meaning. There the lines of defence were perfectly organised behind the earth banks covered with bushes forming ramparts that the soldiers of the 29th and 35th US Inf.Div.

had to negociate, a process constantly repeated. Misery and despair were sometimes the lot of the men who had either to rush towards the enemy, or stop and get hit, or sometimes turn round and get killed with more certainly. The middle of the field was the point of no return, one could only rush to the hedge ahead. As one said: at the rate we are going this blessed war could well last 10 years !

## A. The offensive of the flanks of the 1st Army (5th and 8th Corps).

The 5th Corps which was holding Caumont in the east encountered much difficulty in front of Hill 192 where until the end of June the 2nd US Inf.Div. lost 1200 men in trying to conquer the heights of Clocheville which were bitterly defended by the paratroopers of the 2nd German Corps of General Meindl. The 5th Corps was to stay there for 2 more weeks.

After deadly weeks of slow progress in the Bocage, the US Infantry (opposite page) at last getting near Saint-lô which will be taken on July 18 and 19. Above : On July 19, the 29th Inf. Div. entering the town at Carrefour de La Bascule - eastern entry of the town - to reach the centre of the town where Sherman tanks are firing (below) in the middle of the ruins (US Army photos).

*In Saint-Lô, July 19. Some infantrymen (above) have dug in near Sainte-Croix church. The body of Major Howie (opposite page, bottom) who was killed during the attack on the town, was brought by his men and buried up against the church walls. Some tanks are patrolling along the streets of the old town (opposite page, top). One of the spires of Notre-Dame church is still intact. It was knocked down later on by a German shell. (US Army photos).*

In Saint-Lô, July 19. US Infantry hunting down German snipers house by house, (above). Opposite page, bottom: A GI watching the ruins of the main post-office overlooking the district of La Dollée from the road leading to Pont-Hébert above the northern districts of the town. Opposite page, top: the view from the belfry of Notre-Dame church which was still intact, Saint-Lô, is nothing but ruins. (US Army photos).

The 8th Corps in the west had been assigned the task of reaching Coutances starting from a departure line Saint-Sauveur/Carentan. To carry out this mission it had to take the heights of Mont-Gardon and Mont-Castre overlooking La-Haye-du-Puits. Opposition had been considered as disorganised by US staff. On **July 3** the 90th Division was stopped at Prétot and at the foot of Mont-Castre: they had advanced of 900 metres and had lost 600 men killed. The 79th Inf.Div. was also static before Mont-Gardon, which made people say: the Germans haven't left much, but they know how to use it.

The 90th began the ascent of Mont-Castre on **July 7** but reached its summit 900 metres away only on **July 9**. 2,000 men were the casualties for 6 kilometres gained. Mont-Gardon was mopped up on July 8 by the 79th US Inf.Div. (1500 losses). On the same day the 82nd US Airborne took La-Haye-du-Puits more easily and handed this town over to the 8th US Inf.Div. (General Stroh) which had just landed. La-Haye-du-Puits was the last town to be liberated by US paratroopers. The 82th and 101st Airborne were sent back to England via Utah-Beach on July 13 and 14 to be refitted and get ready for other possible airborne operations.

At the end of the first week of July, General Bradley abandoned all hopes of seeing the 8th Corps reach its objective: the capture of Coutances. He decided that his departure line for his general

*Saint-Lô. Opposite page, top: The face of a German sergeant distorted by pain when he was hoisted into a half-track by GIs to be taken to a field hospital. Bottom of the opposite page : the district of La Dollée at the foot of the old town had become a lunar landscape (US Army photos). Below: the front is now further away from the town: lorries bringing supplies seen here crossing the ruins of the Norman city.*

offensive would be more modest i.e. the road Lessay/Périers/Saint-Lô which had to be reached as soon as possible and to be held firmly.

Eighteen days of slow fastidious advance through the network of the Bocage countryside would be necessary to reach this new position, less than 10 kilometres ahead. On July 10 the 8th Corps was overlooking that road from Mont-Castre. Transfers were made, reprimands for incompetence distributed as 10,000 men had been lost for a gain of 12 kilometres whereas the final objectives was still 3 times that distance away.

## B. The 7th Corps in the Centre (1st to 14th July)

The 3 assault divisions of General Collins regrouped south of Carentan and had to progress along the road from Carentan to Périers. This road which was surrounded by marshes did not offer much possibility for tactical move-ment, it became known as "the isthmus" and was to hamper the operations of the 83rd, the 4th and 9th US Inf.Div. for 2 weeks in this sector. On **July 4** the 83rd division (General Macon) was stopped before Saint-Eny. The 17th SS-Pz. Grenadier-Division reinforced by motorised elements of the 2nd SS-Panzerdivision (Das Reich) rushed from the west of Caen were occupying the ground from Tribehou to Raids, together with the paratroopers of the 6th regiment at Saint-Eny who had fought gallantly ever since June 6. On July 5 the 83rd US Inf.Div. gained 200 metres towards Saint-Eny, captured 6 prisoners and lost at least 1450 men. The following day it won 1500 more metres from the Germans after a deluge of shells from the Corps artillery. It cost the 83rd 750 extra victims. Some medics who had been captured by "Das Reich" during this operation were sent back to General Macon with a note saying that were

After the fall of Saint-Lô roads were badly needed. A team of soldiers clearing a street of mines (opposite page). In the meantime the front was once more fluid further west at Lessay where the 79th Inf. Div. (above and below) made slow progress among the hedgerows. (US Army photos).

certainly more needed by the Americans but that if the fortunes of war changed, the Germans would be pleased to be offered their services...

The 4th US Inf.Div. which had proved its value from Utah-Beach to Cherbourg in June came to support the 83rd on its left. It was not more successful against this German plug in the middle of the isthmus, 1500 metres from Sainteny which would fall only on **July 14**. The losses of the 83rd amounted then to 4700 in 12 days of fighting. The 4th which had more experience suffered only 2400 casualties in 10 days. On **July 15** the 7th Corps left the isthmus to the 8th Corps and went to support the 19th Corps engaged north of Saint-Lô.

## C. The Advance of the 19th Corps towards Saint-Lô (July 1 - 18).

The 19th US Corps of General Corlett had been engaged since the end of June on either side of the road Isigny/Saint-Lô. The outposts of the 29th US Inf.Div. were 8 kilometres in the north east of Saint-Lô and could not progress further. So an attack was launched to outflank the Germans from the west on July 3. It started from the Vire-Taute

canal and was part of the plan of the "general offensive" through the bocage country of the 1st American Army.

On **July 7** the 30th US Inf.Div. (General Hobbs) managed to cross the well defended canal and reached Saint-Jean-de-Daye by the north and the east, then Airel. There the bridges over the River Vire were repaired by the engineers under the fire of the field artillery. This successful operation was carried out by the 30th division with little opposition from the Germans whose main forces were busy mostly around La-Haye-du-Puits and in the "isthmus" at the same time (17th and 2nd SS Divisions) and also in the north east of Saint-Lô (2nd Parachute Corps of General Meindl). This bridgehead at Saint-Jean-de-Daye was exploited by the 3rd US Arm.Div. which tried a breakthrough towards Saint-Lô but became lost in the maze of Bocage and created a frightful mess which allowed the 84th Corps of von Choltitz to close the gap on **July 12**. The "Panzer-Lehr" Division had just arrived in the area of Saint-Lô after leaving the sector of Tilly-sur-Seulles (Chap.A.3). It was reinforced by ele-

*About July 20. Civilians making friends with GIs in front of the ruins of their house (opposite page, US Army photo). Above: a first aid post for German infantry between Périers and Lessay (Bundesarchiv).*

ments of the 2nd SS-Panzerdivision ("Das Reich") and a brigade on bicycles attached to the "Panzer-Lehr". This division was not what it used to be for, as early as June 26, out of the 190 tanks belonging to Pz.Regt. 130 on June 6, only 66 could be counted as roadworthy. On July 1st 36 "Model IV" and 32 "Panther" could be used. This armoured counterattack towards the bridgehead of Saint-Jean-de-Daye threatened for a whole day the American frontline held by the 30th US Inf.Div. and the Combat Command B of the 3rd US Arm.Div. But because of the attacks of the fighter-bombers and of the US artillery it could not break through the American lines and withdrew to a defensive position north of the road Saint-Lô/Périers.

In 9 days of fightings the 30th US Inf.Div. had lost 3,300 men and gained 13 kilometres of Norman land whereas the 9th US Inf.Div. which had been lent by the 7th Corps and had more experience left 2,500 victims along the 9 kilometres it had gained in 6 days of fighting.

On **July 15** the 7th Corps took over the sector of Saint-Jean-de-Daye to the west of Saint-Lô and the 19th Corps went to its left, the road Carentan/Saint-Lô being the border between the 2 Corps. The town of Saint-Lô was now the symbol of all the efforts of the GIs who had been fighting around its wall for a fortnight. The schedule of the 1st American Army had forseen its capture on D+9. But this was without taking the obstinate resistance of the 2nd German Parachute Corps into account. On **July 11** the 35th US Inf.Div. (General Baade)could see the outskirts of the town from Hill 122, 1500 metres away while the 29th US Inf.Div. of General Gerhardt was conquering slowly the heights of Martinville in the north east at the cost of 1000 casualties in two days. In the **evening of July 15** the companies of the 115th Regiment of the 29th Inf.Div. were reduced to 35 to 50 men instead of 185 in the beginning. On **July 18th** at 5.30 p.m. this same regiment progressed through the ruins of Saint-Lô from the east (La Madeleine) while

*There was a bitter struggle for Lessay. Opposite page: two German infantrymen running during an assault (Bundesarchiv). The small town wax taken of July 27 by the 79th US Inf. Div. This young German soldier who was killed at the entrance of the town (above) might well be one of those seen running in the previous photo (YS Army photo).*

the 116th Regiment, organised as a task force including infantry, tanks, engineers and artillery, entered Saint-Lô from the north after 43 days of continuous fighting from Omaha-Beach which had cost to the 29th and 35th US Inf.Div. 7,000 casualties.

The body of an officer of the 115th Inf.Rgt. was deposited on the ruins of Sainte-Croix church. He had the American flag as a shroud. The supreme sacrifice of Major Howie had been chosen to symbolise the sufferings of the American liberators in the war of the hedgerows ending in the ruins of Saint-Lô.

**Visiting the area.**

One can go to Saint-Lô via Carentan and Saint-Jean-de-Daye where at a crossroads 1 kilometre south of the town one can take the road D.8 to **Le Dézert**. There one can see a German 50mm antitank gun. The villages have been rebuilt since 1950-1960. In **Saint-Lô** one can go to Place du Major Howie, a roundabout with a road going to Bayeux. There stands a monument to Major Howie commemorating also the sacrifice of 8,000 G.Is.

# B.4. The breakthrough and the advance of the US Army to the West of Saint-Lô: Operation Cobra. July 24 to August 1, 1944.

After 4 weeks of static war the 1st American Army had now an excellent base large enough to accomodate its four Army Corps which would soon be reinforced by three more Corps forming the 3rd Army of General Patton. The time had now come for the big breakthrough which would transform the exhausting hedgerows war into a "Blitzkrieg". This was the object of Operation Cobra which would take the American tanks and infantrymen in 6 days from the Saint-Lô/Périers road to Avranches and the bridge over River Sélune at Pontaubault, opening the roads to Brittany.

The Americans were to break through a front 7 kilometres wide which was held by the "Panzer-Lehr" Division rein-

*Cobra. On july 25 a fantastic carpet of bombs wiped out what was left of the "Panzer-Lehr" Armd. Div. and the 2nd and 3rd US Army. Div. were then able to rush into the gap opened in the German front. Opposite page: the ruins of Hébécrevon on the Saint-Lô-Périers road. Above: a concentration of tanks and GIs ready for battle. Below: a column of GIs crossing Courson on July 25 (US Army photos).*

*Cobra. Saint-Gilles was in the centre of the carpet of bombs which produced the breakthrough. Opposite page, top: the infantry of the 35th US Inf. Div. passing in front of the ruins of the church. Above and bottom of opposite page: the "Mark IV" tanks of the "Panzer-Lehr" were turned upside down by 500 1b bombs of the 9th US Air Force. These tanks belonged to the 5th company. (US Army Photos).*

*July 27. Above: Marigny is now free, some American vehicles are parked on the market square of the now silent town. Opposite page: 2 Norman people returning home. Such destruction had not been since the Hundred Years War (US Army photos).*

Cobra. The breakthrough was a success. Above: a tank of the 4th US Armd. Div. taking position in Périers to support the right wing of the offensive. Below: 1.3 kilometre from La Bellangerie and 2.5 km from Montreuil-L'Argillé, a well camouflaged tank-destroyed mounting guard at a crossroads, near the wrecks of a German half track and a 88mm gun. Opposite page, top: the crew of an M8 armoured car being offered a glass of local cider near Périers. Bottom: On July 28, the columns of the 4th US Army Armd. Div. crossing Saint-Sauveur-Lendelin towards Coutances. (US Army photos).

Above: Coming from Périers and Saint-Sauveur-Lendelin, the 4th US Armd. Div. was getting near Coutances on July 28. Below: the vanguard of this unit, sergeant Vincent Morana of New York and private William Melchiori of Flushing (Ohio) on the outskirts of the town which was taken on July 29. Opposite page: Outside the cathedral one of the priests explains to an American officer how the inhabitants have left the town to find refuge in the countryside and to escape the dreadful bombing. Coutances was a bottleneck for German troops retreating from the Lessay area. (US Army photos).

*Opposite page, top: along the Coutances to Saint-Gilles road. Civilians are now returning to their villages hoping to find their houses undamaged while US ambulances are driving towards the front line. On July 29, there were still infantry skirmishes on the outskirts of Coutances (opposite page, bottom). After the fighting this "Stuart" light tank (above) was wrecked by a land mine in Coutances. This sort of incident was frequent on the road from Périers which was mined. This German military cemetery (below) shows how fierce the battles were in this sector. (US Army photos).*

But on July 29 Coutances was outflanked to the south east; the 2nd US Armd. Div. was at Saint-Denis-le-Gast and Lengronne on July 28 closing the trap at Roncey. Some German elements managed to escape during the night of July 28-29, the others were caught after a final struggle. Above: SS-Grenadiers of the "Götz von Berlichingen" Division taken prisoner and four other Germans (below) near Roncey. Opposite page: the equipment captured was plentiful: guns in front of the school of Roncey (top), a half track of "Das Reich" and self propelled guns (bottom). More than 150 vehicles of that type were captured here. (US Army photos).

147

*Opposite page: At Roncey, GIs mustering prisoners. One can see German officers of the 3rd Parachute Div. and of the 2nd SS-Panzerdivision facing the Americans of the 2nd US Armd. Div. The same units but on opposite sides ! Bottom: near the church of Roncey, the wrecks of other German vehicles - a "Schwimmwagen", a half-track, two self propelled guns and other sundry vehicles (US Army and author's coll.). On July 30, the American troops were at La Lucerne-d'Outremer (above and below). Two Carmelite nuns of Avranches, Sister Anna-Joceph and Sister Emilia, acted as go-betweens for the surrender of a group of wounded German paratroopers and their medics to the soldiers of the 4th US Armd. Div. thus probably saving their lives. (US Army photos).*

From Coutances to Avranches.
Above: Saint-Denis-le-Gast was taken on July 25. A photographer of the 1st US Army and his companion. Below: At Bréhal, some civilians taking a war trophy away. Opposite page: Gavray was taken on July 30, the very day when the advanced elements of the 4th US Armd. Div. arrived at Avranches. Top Picture: a "Panther" tank has toppled over into a ravine near Gavray at the beginning of August. The bridge at Gavray had been destroyed by the retreating Germans. The American engineers built another one (bottom of page) to allow their vehicles across the river Sienne. (US Army photos).

forced by a regiment of the 5th German Parachute Division. The 9th US Airforce dropped a carpet of bombs 1500 metres deep: 5,000 tons of medium bombs were dropped by some 2,000 heavy bombers: Liberators and Flying Fortresses which annihilated the armour and the paratroopers. The 7th Corps launched its assault battalions. Some of them had suffered casualties caused by American bombs falling inside American lines. The losses amounted to 500. But, in spite of the chaos on the ground churned up by explosions which had created ten of thousands of craters, it was still necessary to fight to capture this moon-like area. As for the "Panzer-Lehr", after such a hurricane of fire, none of the 40 tanks of Pz.Lehr.Regt

130 that this unit possessed at the beginning of the bombing, was left intact. Some had been thrown upside down, others had fallen down into bomb craters. But the German workshop worked frantically to such good effect that the 130th tank Rgt managed to muster 14 tanks at Canisy. 14 more tanks joined them before the 3rd US Armd. Div. and 1st US Inf.Div. could start marching towards Coutances. But that was not much to slow down the advance of the American armour.

The 4th Inf.Div. attacked in the centre towards Marigny and Saint-Gilles. It had the 9th US Inf.Div. on its left and the 30th on its right. 6,000 men of the "Panzer-Lehr" and the regiment of paratroo-

*Avranches. The town was captured by the 4th US Armd. Div. on July 30. Taking advantage of the situation it reached Pontaubault and Ducey on the 31st and fanned out towards Brittany and Maine. Opposite: The wrecks of German vehicles in what is now Boulevard de Luxembourg on the road out of Avranches. Above: a long column of German prisoners crossing Pont-Gilbert - a suburb of Avranches - on July 31 towards a POW camp. (US Army photos).*

153

*Above: the 4th US Armd. Div. reached the fortified area of Saint-Malo on August 5. Meanwhile, coming from Avranches, this patrol could admire Mont-Saint-Michel. Below: motorised and horsedrawn German vehicles could be seen destroyed or abandoned along the road leading from Avranches to Mortain. Opposite page: GIs of the 119th Inf. Regt. advancing near Juvigny-le-Tertre.*

pers had been wiped out around La-Chapelle-Enjuger and Hébécrevon, but some pockets of resistance had to be bypassed then eliminated. So precious hours were lost in fierce combats giving time to other German units further away from the battle to recover and to find counter measures to the offensive of the 7th US Corps.

On the evening of **July 25th** the atmosphere was rather gloomy at the headquarters of General Bradley: the Périers/Saint-Lô road had been reached (4th Inf.Div.) but Marigny and Saint-Gilles were still far ahead. General Bradley has admitted in his memoirs that dejection had fallen on them like a black fog;

On **July 26th**, General Collins launched the units of his assault divisions selected for the attack - the 1st Inf.Div.

and Combat Command B of the 3rd US Armd.Div. reached Marigny once the main line of resistance had been pierced and Combat Command B of the 2nd US Armd.Div. reached Canisy at the end of the day, overtaking helpless Germans on the roads. On **July 27** in spite of the fierce resistance of combat groups of the 2nd and 17th SS divisions, the Combat Command B of the 3rd US Armd.Div. supported by the 1st US Inf.Div. gained 8 kilometres south west of Marigny and reached Cerisy-la-Salle.

In the meantime the 8th Corps was progressing from Périers/Lessay towards Coutances which was now directly threatened. The idea was to contain the bulk of the German forces there so that the 7th Corps could cut them off south of Coutances and make them capitulate.

General von Choltitz who commanded the 84th Corps understood the threat and ordered his troops to withdraw in good order towards the south. When the 1st US Inf.Div. and the tanks of the 3rd Us Armd.Div. cut the Coutances/Granville road on **July 29** having covered 14 kilometres in a day without any serious opposition, it was too late. The "big fish" had escaped from the net. Only some mixed groups of SS and paratoopers were left behind to slow down the advance around Coutances. This gave 36 more hours for the 84th Corps to achieve its strategic retreat. When the 4th US Armd.Div. entered Coutances on **July 30** the Germans had disappeared leaving behind them plenty of mines and boody-traps. The 3 German divisions which were retreating towards the south east were intercepted by US fighter-bombers in and around the village of Roncey on July 28 et 29.

500 vehicles including 100 tanks were destroyed. The 2nd US Armd.Div. managed to encircle 2,700 men belonging mostly to the 2nd and 17th SS Div. and 1,500 more were captured in an ambush at Saint-Denis-le-Gast. At Cérences in a pitched battle which lasted 8 hours US tank-destroyers opposed retreating Germans. Here the Germans lost 450 dead, 1000 prisoners and 150 vehicles. The American breakthrough across the Bocage after a difficult start was now in full swing. It was now exploited by the 3rd Army of General Patton on the 30th. He let loose the 4th and 6th US Armd.Div. straight from Coutances to Avranches. His aim was not to let the Germans recover and to prevent them from reorganising their front without bothering about his left flank. This was not protected for 20 kilometres due to the slow progress of the 7th Corps which was advancing methodically and

*On August 7 the Germans launched a counter attack at Mortain aimed at cutting off the American Army. Their offensive was slowed down by the 30th US Inf. Div. and then crushed by the Air Force. After the German failure (above) a lot of vehicles were destroyed and abandoned near the railway station of Mortain. In the foreground one can see a car of the 2nd Panzerdivision (the trident painted on the body was its recognition mark). All the sides of the roads leading to Mortain were jammed with the wrecks of the vehicles (opposite page): a half track of a SS Division, a "Schwimmwagen" etc..(US Army photos).*

157

facing an enemy as aggressive as in the bocage around Saint-Lô in early July from La-Haye-Pesnel to Percy. The left flank of the 7th Corps of General Collins was also exposed by the slow progress of the 19th and 5th Corps which were entangled in the bocage and where facing the 2nd German parachute Corps in the area Tessy/Torigny-sur-Vire where they lost 1,800 men in 4 days. The battle raged around Tessy from July 27 to 31. The 29th, 30th and 35th US Inf.Div. did their best while facing the German anti-tank guns and automatic weapons hidden behind the hedgerows. Tessy was captured in the evening of **August 1st**. This allowed the 19th Corps to push towards Vire.

When the tanks of the 4th US Armd.Div. reached Pontaubault on August 1st, they found the bridge intact. The road to Brittany was now open to the 3rd Army. The 5th US Corps in the east had covered 11 kilometres in 6 days, the 7th 45 kilometres, the 8th more than 80 kilometres in the same time thanks to the thrust of its brand new powerful motorised units. Day and night the stream of vehicles of the 15th, 12th and 20th Corps followed bumper to bumper, roaring through the bottle-neck Avranches/Pontaubault which was the vital artery of the Norman front. In 10 days the Battle of Normandy was to become the Battle of France.

**Places to visit:**
- The German military cemetery of **Marigny** at La Chapelle-Enjuger (11,169 graves)
- At **Jullouville-les-Pins** a monument recalls that General Eisenhower had his headquarters in that place in August 1944.
- At **Landelles et Coupigny** a plaque commemorates the 29th US Inf.Div. which liberated the village in the beginning of August 1944.

*Opposite page: the advanced HQ of the 30th US Inf. Div. near Domfront. Above: German prisoners walking through Domfront. Below: In Barenton. Some elements of the 2nd French Armd. Div. talking with local population. These men are wearing the camouflage overalls of the American Army which were not much used because of a possible confusion with similar German outfits. (US Army photos).*

- At **Avranches**, a monument commemorates General Patton and his 3rd Army.
- The bridge at **Pontaubault** crossed by 100,000 vehicles in August 1944.
- The German military cemetery (ossuary) at Huisnes (11,956 graves)
- The US military cemetery of Saint-James (4,410 graves).

# B.5. The US exploitation of Cobra and the German counterattack at Mortain: Operation Liege, August 2 to 12 1944.

On **August 1st**, Hitler who was giving orders directly from his headquarters in East Prussia ordered Army Group B in Normandy to counterattack with all forces available towards Avranches and cut off the American advance. The fate of the campaign of France rested on the success of this offensive. But in his message of July 10 Montgomery maintained that the enemy could do what they wanted, his own plan would not be changed. This is exactly what happened in the early days of August: the 1st Canadian Army of Crear was attacking from Troarn to May-sur-Orne, the 2nd British Army was carrying on its great offensive from Saint-Martin-des-Besaces to the Vassy/Vire road, the 1st US Army of Hodges - who had succeded Bradley who was now at the head of the 12th US Army Group - was fighting the 2nd German Parachute Corps clinging to the bocage around Vire and the 47th Armoured Corps in the area Tessy/Percy. And while all that was going on the 3rd Army of Patton had been selected by Montgomery for the pursuit. Montgomery knew full well how clever and audacious a man Patton was - he embodied the real spirit of armoured warfare regarding speed as more important than security: he was the right man for the present task, a pursuit in the old traditions of the cavalry charges which would not allow the enemy to recover.

On **August 1** between Avranches and Pontaubault Patton delivered a body blow (4th US Armd.Div.) to the 77th German Inf.Div. which was heading towards Avranches to plug the gap. It left 250 vehicles along the winding R.N. 176 in the outskirts of Avranches. Then the 6th US Armd.Div. sped towards Pontorson and Rennes allowing the 8th Corps to drive towards Brest while the 12th Corps was speeding towards the River Loire, the 20th towards Orléans and the 15th towards the River Seine which was reached on J +75 i.e. 15 days in advance of the plan. This fantastic exploitation of Operation Cobra was really a race against the clock, the aim of which was to drive the Germans out of Brittany, capture the ports necessary for the unloading of urgent supplies and then to encircle between the rivers Seine and Loire all the German forces fighting in Normandy and capture them.

But at the beginning of August the situation was far from desperate for the Germans if we except the sector of the breakthrough at Avranches. The 7th Army with its 3 Army Corps was still something to reckon with and the 5th Armd.Army would incorporate the 1st and 2nd SS Armd.Corps still formidable units though reduced in men and machines. It also included 5 infantry divisions and the 9th Panzer which were now trying to reach the Norman front to obey the Führer's orders.

On **August 3rd** the 1st US Inf.Div. occupied Mortain and resistance became stiffer on the front of the 7th and 19th US Corps. These progressed only at the rate of 2 or 3 kilometres a day and losses increased too. The 15th Corps of the 3rd Army reached Fougères on **August 5**, Mayenne and Laval on the 6th and Le Mans on the **9th** cutting off German communication lines behind the front. There was a gap 30 kilometres wide between the 1st Army at Mortain and the 3rd Army at Mayenne. There the Germans had freedom of movement except for the constant threat of being attacked by air. During the **night of August 6/7** from Sourdeval to Barenton,

4 Panzerdivisionen launched a joint attack - it was unexpected for there had been no previous artillery support. This was the first large scale German counter offensive towards the sea on Norman soil (Operation Liege). This assault given by 200 tanks supported by combat groups of 3 infantry divisions in early morning was successfull all through the day on **August 7**. 9 kilometres were covered westwards. Mortain was recaptured from the 30 US Inf.Div. but on **August 8**, American defences which had given way were now once more active with the help of the rockets of the "Typhoons" of the 2nd Tactical Air Force of the RAF. These knocked out 115 tanks and armoured vehicles around Mortain between August 8 and 11 forcing the Germans to dig in. The battle turned into a series of clashes between small units. Then from **August 12** the Germans progressively withdrew their

*Below: This was the Hôtel de la Poste in Mortain. In the département of La Manche 280,000 people out of a population of 438,000 were made homeless by bombing. 68 % of the farm buildings were either damaged or destroyed in Calvados and La Manche. 40,000 hectares of arable land were temporarily made useless.*

troops when they realised that they were in great danger of being encircled and that their armour would soon have supply problems.

From August 8 to 12 the fighting around Mortain caused 4,300 losses in the 3rd US Corps. The total of the American losses since the landings amonted to 102,000 on August 11, compared with 68,000 in the British sector.

# B.6. The US pursuit and the German retreat in the Mortain-Argentan pocket. 12 to 17 August 1944.

On August 11 General Montgomery said that all the energy of the Allies should be concentrated on closing the gap behind the German army and that it was possible to destroy it where it then stood.

On **August 10** the 90th and 79th US Inf.Div., the 5th US Armd.Div. and the 2nd French Armd.Division of General Leclerc under the command of the 15th Corps of General Haislip reached Le Mans. The German commander had hastily evacuated his installations and thrown the 81st Corps - mostly horsedrawn - across the route of the 15th US Corps. The Germans were destroyed. On **August 12** General Leclerc could give his orders from the bridges on the River Sarthe at Alençon and the 5th US Armd.Div. (General Oliver) entered Sées. On **August 13 in the evening** the 2nd French Armd.Div. had finished clearing Forêt d'Ecouves where the main part of the 9th Panzer had been intercepted and destroyed. While progressing towards Carrouges and Argentan the French constantly encountered German motorised units retreating from Mortain,

mainly in Ecouché where 300 SS were decimated. On **August 13** a French patrol reached Argentan which was only taken a week later though it was within reach of the French division. General Bradley had overestimated the remaining strength of the 200,000 Germans who were then concentrated in the Mortain-Argentan-Falaise pocket. The Canadians were 10 kilometres from Falaise, with Argentan as their further objective at the southern limit of the sector of the 1st Canadian Army. So on August 13 Haislip received an order from Bradley asking him to stop his advance northwards so as not to bump into the Canadians. His 15th Corps remained static in the vicinity of Argentan from August 13 to 16. His troops were satisfied with intercepting the Germans going east across the road from Argentan to Alençon. On **August 17** Falaise was cleared by the 2nd Canadian Inf.Div. while the 1st Polish Armd.Div. was making progress in the hills of Pays d'Auge above Trun, with Chambois as their objective. The 30th and 8th British Corps were advancing from Condé to Putanges, the 5th US Corps took Tinchebray on August 15, the 19th had taken Domfront the day before and drove through Flers on August 16. On August 17 the 7th US Corps reached the Flers-Argentan road at Fromentel and captured 3000 prisoners. On August 15 Field-marshall von Kluge ordered all German forces still fighting west of the River Orne to cross over it. It was obvious that the only solution left to the German troops hard-pressed on all sides and harassed by the Air Force was either to escape or to surrender if they did not want to fall under the hail of bullets, bombs and shells of the Allies.

But when the order was given to the Canadians and the Americans on

**August 18** to close the gap and seal the pocket between Trun and Chambois, this lack of judgement of the allied High Command had allowed some 100,000 Germans to leave the pocket between August 13 and 17. The 15th Corps abandoned its "road police duty" at Argentan and resumed its path to glory - to Paris. It lent the 90th Inf.Div. and a part of the 2nd Armd.Div. to the 5th US Corps of Gerow who was in charge of the southern jaw of the vice, from Argentan to Bourg-Saint-Léonard where the 90th Div. managed to seize and keep the crossroads they had lost 4 times in 2 days. The allied troops were now all around the pocket and, with their mutual protection guaranteed, they constantly applied pressure on the 100,000 German soldiers who sought to leave Normandy alive. All that was left was to put the lid on the seething cauldron and capture those who remained.

**Places to visit:**

- Between Alençon and Sées, a monument along RN 138 to commemorate the 2nd French Armoured Division of General Leclerc.

- In Forêt d'Ecouves, a Sherman tank commemorates the fighting of August 13 at the crossroads of Croix de Médevi.

- At Saint-Christophe-de-Jajolet a Sherman tank of the 501st Tank Regiment of the 2nd Armd.Div. has been left where it was hit by a Panzerfaust on August 14. A monument recalls the sacrifice of its crew who were born in Alençon.

---

*At Chambois, on August 24, some GIs and Poles riding horses taken from the German. The civilians are back home. (US Army photos).*

163

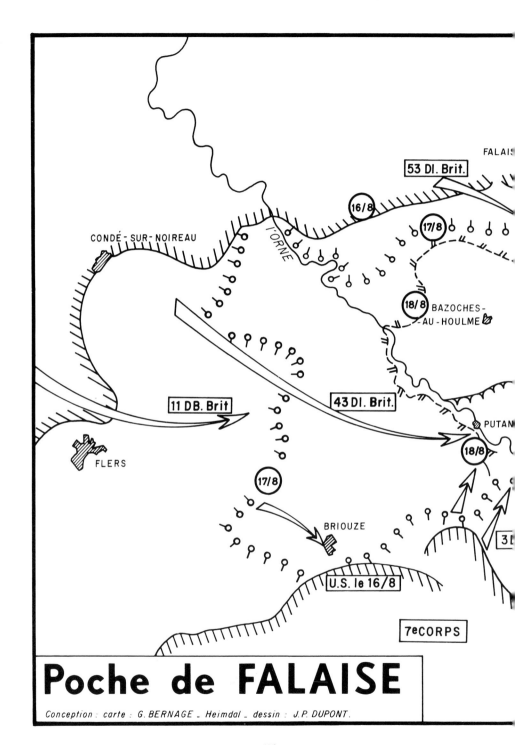

# Poche de FALAISE

Conception : carte : G. BERNAGE _ Heimdal _ dessin : J.P. DUPONT.

164

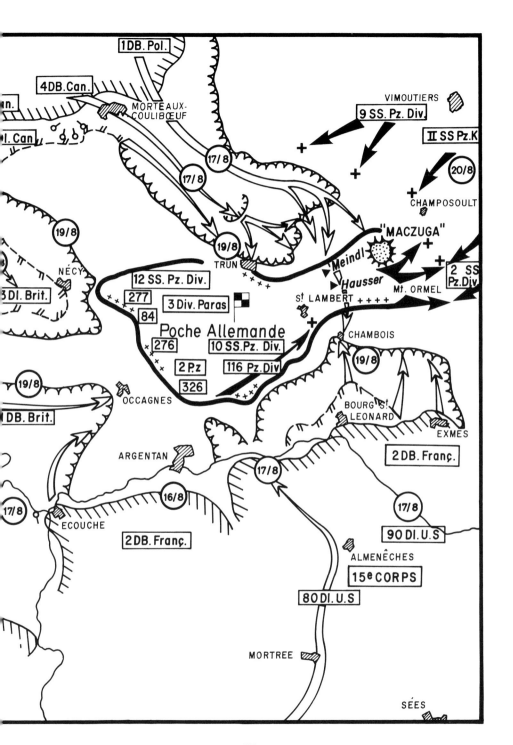

# THE FALAISE POCKET

## 1. CLOSING THE POCKET.

In the evening of August 17, under the heavy pressure of the American armies in the south, the British armies in the west, and the Canadians in the north, the badly mauled divisions of the German 7th Army and the 5th German Armoured Army were confined in an area 30 kilometres long by 15 kilometres wide. In this "pocket" there were some 100,000 Germans unmercifully pounded by the shells and bombs: they were what was left of 15 divisions and the stragglers of a dozen more divisions. The only way out was the narrow roads crossing the River Dives between Trun and Chambois under the fire of allied artillery and their air forces. The fighter-bombers of the 2nd Tactical Air-Force eargerly strafed convoys all through those sunny days of August. The Spitfires were waiting their turn and as soon as the Typhoons had fired their last anti-tank rockets, they would join in to spray the roads, lanes and hedges with bullets. Near Damblainville one could even see a group of P.51 fighter-bombers capture a German infantry battalion and hold it captive until the arrival of the Canadian tanks.

But the convergence of three Allied armies on such a narrow sector, all with a common objective, inevitably meant losses as men made mistakes in the identification of troops and machines - sometimes at only a few dozen metres distance.

**Friday August 18.**
The 15th US Corps formed the southern jaw of the Allied vice with its 80th Inf.Div. around Argentan, the 90th Inf.Div. at Bourg-Saint-Léonard and the French 2nd Armd.Div. at Exmes.

The 12th British Corps in the west was pushing the Germans into the pincers. In the north the 2nd Canadian Corps had been ordered by Montgomery to join the American forces at Chambois and firmly establish their line of defence on the River Dives. The idea was to close the last escape routes of the Germans. The staff at the allied GHQ were quite optimistic: the only thing left was to round up the prisoners and take possession of their equipment.

This order applied specifically to the 1st Polish Armd.Div. which during the night of August 17-18 had captured Champeaux by mistake, its civilian guide not understanding the Polish accent had mistaken this place for Chambois. The 8th Rifles (Polish) ransacked the Headquarters of the 2nd SS Armd.Div. "Das Reich". A furious fight followed where, according to General Maczek commander of Polish Division "God thus gave us the chance to take revenge on that unit which had fought in Poland in 1939, but this time the roles were reversed". The Polish armoured column reached Coudehard at daybreak where retreating Germans crowded together. To deal with this force, the 2nd Polish Armoured Regiment the 8th Rifles and anti-tank batteries regrouped on Hill 262, north of Mont-Ormel where they could control the whole valley of the River Dives and the roads which carried a continuous flow of Germans going due east towards Vimoutiers and the River Seine but also heading straight towards the Poles. A mixed column, of both horsedrawn and motorised vehicles was struggling up the hill of road D 16 (Chambois-Vimoutiers): the horses slowing down the

*Above: Briefing of the 24th Polish Lancers in August 1944; Opposite page: a reconnaissance element of the 1st Polish Armd. Div. near Champosoult on August 17 (Photos Doc. française).*

167

march. In less than 15 minutes it was cut to pieces by the intensive fire of the Poles. The Germans then discovered with terror that their retreat route was henceforth cut off. They began to fire mortars at Hill 262 in the morning and continued for two days to try to drive off or anihilate the Polish force occupying this strategic hill.

*A Canadian "Mustang" on photographic reconnaissance flying over Clinchamp. A German armoured column can be seen on the road. Above: retreating German units going across country to avoid the jams on the road. They formed ideal targets for Allied pilots. (IWM photos).*

At 10 a.m. the last SS left Trun with the tanks of the 4th Canadian Armd.Div. on their heels. Its reconnaissance regiment was ready to move towards Chambois too with its Squadron C - 15 tanks and 130 fusilliers of Co B of the "Argyll and Sutherland Highlanders of Canada" - under the command of Major D.V. Currie. The latter had been ordered to cut off the retreat of the 7th German Army on the River Dives with his small force. He was to take the bridges at Saint-Lambert and then contact the Americans at Chambois. Currie's Tactical Group did reach Saint-Lambert in the evening at 7 o'clock. The leading tank was immediately destroyed by an anti-tank gun placed at the crossroads in the village. Because of this operation, Major Currie was awarded the Victoria Cross, the highest decoration of the British Empire. His tactical group prepared to spend the night at the entrance of the town on a hill overlooking the place.

At this stage, the pocket was only 9 kilometres wide by 12 kilometres long. It contained the following German units:

a) The Headquarters of the 7th Army of General Hausser, and the Eberbach Armoured Group, HQ of the 74th Army Corps (von Funck), 84th Corps (Elfeld), 47th Armoured Corps(Staube) and 2nd Para Corps (Meindl).

b) What was left of the 84th, 226th, 227th, 326th, 353rd, 363rd Inf.Div. the 3rd Div. of Riflemen-Paratroopers, the armoured divisions (exhausted and depleted by two months of fighting) belonging to the 1st SS-Panzerdivision, the 10th SS-Panzerdivision, the 12th SS-Panzerdivision, the 2nd Panzerdivision and the 116th Panzerdivision.

c) The services and supply convoys, groups of stragglers and lost men showing the symptoms of "Kesselfieber" -

the panic at being surrounded as they approached the River Dives, just as had enveloped them at Stalingrad. Some groups were trying to stop fighting at all cost, others would do their utmost to find an exit. The men wounded or simply exhausted dragged themselves along like cattle.

At noon, the 2nd SS-Panzer-Corps of General Bittrich evacuated his two key divisions the 2nd and the 9th SS-Panzerdivisionen in good order by the roads to Trun and Chambois to Vimoutiers. There had been a rumour among the Wehrmacht that the SS were running away, clearing the way, pistols in hand. The truth was different: the 2nd Armoured Corps was to reach Vimoutiers as soon as possible to be reconstituted and then return to the pocket to fight the Poles who were guarding the exit, to prevent Canadians linking up with the Americans and to allow the remnants of the two retreating German armies to escape.

At 8 p.m. on August 18 it became impossible to escape via Trun, the escape route was blocked at Mont-Ormel on road D 16. Chambois was under American observation at Bourg

and under French observation at Omméel and Saint-Lambert while the Canadian tactical force was keeping close watch on the bridges. They had to follow secondary roads going over the River Dives at and around Saint-Lambert and Moissy and then up the slopes of the hills of Pays d'Auge, Neauphe, Coudehard, Boisjos, Mont-Ormel always under the close watch of the Polish Armd.Division.

### Saturday August 19.

In the centre of the pocket, the village of Tournai-sur-Dives - 400 inhabitants - was the crossroads of evacuation routes for German artillery. Allied artillery fire began suddenly at 9.30 a.m. and did not let up for 57 hours with 350 guns firing non-stop on the houses and the streets of the village. The dazed civilians, including many refugees from the neighbourhood, tried to escape from that hell and about a hundred of them managed to reach the mill of Saint-Lambert where the Canadians had just set up an outpost. For an hour things were relatively quiet there. But a German convoy of armoured vehicles arrived and attacked the Canadian infantry who had to give ground as German pressure became too severe. The civilians attempted once more to escape, some towards Trun, others towards Chambois always under fire.

In Saint-Lambert the Currie Group made some progress in spite of having two tanks destroyed. The Germans were swarming like ants all over the place surprised to find themselves face to face with Canadians.

700 prisoners were sent to Trun during the day after being ambushed in the streets or caught in the convoys

*Above: German vehicles abandoned during the retreat east of the River Orne and set on fire by Allied fighter-bombers. Opposite page: In Argentan on August 21, a "Panther" wrecked near Saint-Germain church (IWM photos).*

along the main road. But soon the Canadians had to fall back because they were outnumbered. It was possible to see their tanks turning round and round, firing at each other in order to disloge the Germans from the turrest who were trying to fix explosives charges. On several occasions Currie had to order his own artillery to fire at his own positions to disorganize the German assaults and clear the bridges of Saint-Lambert. Currie's Group finally halted near Hill 117 1,000 metres to the north west of Saint-Lambert, as it was impossible to carry out its mission under existing conditions.

At Mont-Ormel, on the ridge where Hills 262 north and south are like the head of a club, the 2nd Polish Armd.Regt. withstood the assaults of the 2nd SS-Panzerdivision on the northern slope and those of the retreating groups on the southern slope. The 1st Polish regiment destroyed more columns of vehicles progressing towards their position with deadly efficacy.

At 7 p.m. the 24th Polish Lancers and the 10th Polish Dragoons coming down from the "Maczuga" - club in Polish -, entered Chambois. At 7,20 p.m. they met the 2nd battalion of the 359th US Inf.Regt. of the 90th US Inf.Div. who had arrived already. The long waited for link up was now a reality, but the position had to be maintained. The whole area between Tournay, Chambois and Mont-Ormel was a seething mass of thousands of Germans and their equipment, still commanded by their officers, harrassed by the fighter-bombers. The pocket was shrinking quickly.

All day long, the Allies complained of being fired at by their neighbours in spite of a "no fire line". The Polish gunners on Hill 262, the Canadians on Hill 117, the French at Omméel the Americans at Fel-Gouffern discovered a continuous succession of ideal targets and the firing orders remained the same for 24 hours until, the roads being made impassable by the accumulated debris and obstructions of all sorts, the Germans were compelled to go cross country.

*Above: German prisoners escorted by Canadians between Falaise and Trun on August 17 (PAC). Opposite page: a Senegalese of the Régiment de Marche du Tchad of the 2nd French Armd. div. proudly showing this german officer captured near Omméel on August 21. (US Army photo).*

In that one day, the 90 US Inf. Div. of General McLain captured 5000 prisoners, killed a considable number of Germans, took or destroyed hundreds of vehicles and tanks. It had joined up with the Poles and met the Canadians.

The night of August 19/20 was alive with the noise of the German traffic going towards Coudehard and Vimoutiers. The Poles were firing with all their weapons non-stop. Their guns became red hot.

The pocket was sealed, and the battle of the pocket could begin.

## 2. THE BATTLE OF THE POCKET.
### Sunday August 20th.

*a) The crossing of the River Dives around Saint-Lambert/Moissy.*

All day long the Germans fought furiously to hold the bridges of Saint-Lambert in spite of the Canadian artillery firing point blank for the first time in the campaign. All day long the Allies tried unsuccessfully to meet there. Everything was converging towards those three bridges and the fighting there was the bloodiest of the battle.

Carrying out the orders received from OKW the day before by the 7th Army, General Hausser, who was the commander in chief of the troops caught in the trap, organized the evacuation during the night of the majority of the troops and equipment still coming from the west.

Before dawn, General Meindl, commander of the 2nd Corps of Paratroopers, infiltrated the Canadian lines at Saint-Lambert, using a compass with his men following him in total silence. In Indian file under the cover of fog and

Above: German anti aircraft guns (20mm) mounted on half tracks destroyed at Tournay-sur-Dives (author's coll.). Below: A small part of the German equipment accumulated near Moulin de Saint-Lambert-sur-Dives which could not cross the river on August 19-20. Opposite page: German vehicles wrecked at the crossroads of Tournai/Villedieu-les-Bailleul (IWM photos).

darkness. His 2,000 paratroopers were at Coudehard 9.30 a.m. They made several assaults uncoordinated without support on the ridges held by the Poles. The paratroopers were decimated by machine-gun fire. But a gap had been created by Meindl from Saint-Lambert to Coudehard, and by Mahlmann, the commander of the 353th Inf.Div. from Moissy - to Mont-Ormel. This gap was later given the dismal name of "Death Corridor".

On the Canadian side Currie's group could see waves of infantrymen at about 8 a.m. advancing towards their positions on Hill 117 and the nearby areas. "One could not say that it was really an attack there was no support fire : it was rather a rush of infantrymen who were mowed down by the Browning machine guns of the tanks of the Regimental Headquarters. "In Saint-Lambert the report was just the same, but the Canadian soldiers, overwhelmed by the number the German assailants were saved by Squadron A of the "South Alberta" reinforced by a company of the "Lincoln and Welland" who were most welcome.

*Above: heaps of wrecks at Saint-Lambert (author's coll.). Opposite page: more wrecks at Chambois (IWM).*

At Chambois, the 3rd Battalion of the 359th US Inf. Regt. was momentarily driven off its positions by the powerful pressure of German groups who, in reality were not attacking them, but were trying to get away. They were elements driven out by small arm fire and pounded by the artillery of Langlade Tactical Group of the 2nd French Armd.Div. at Omméel and Exmes. They were compelled to abandon all their equipment along the roads.

But on August 20, taking advantage of poor weather conditions. the larger part of the German forces managed to extricate themselves from the shambles. They were the 2nd Parachute Corps (Meindl) from Saint-Lambert to Coudehard, the 47th Armd Corps (von Funck) from Moissy-Chambois to Mont-Ormel,

the 84th Corps (Elfeld) at Moissy was caught by a Polish armoured detachment positioned on Hill 113 in the northwest of Chambois after having used up its ammunition.

The 74th Corps (Straube) and the HQ of the 7th Army with its commanding general and 45,000 men crossed or were waiting to cross the river at the bridges of Saint-Lambert.

The 2nd SS Armd.Corps with its 40 tanks and 3 infantry battalions attracted the attention of the Poles to the north by repeated attacks and cutting off their supply lines, recovering those who were running away.

By noon, Meindl had managed to establish a bridgehead at Coudehard. His headquaters had been set up at la Cour du Bosc where he organized Com-

*Above, top: a horsedrawn column was destroyed in the death corridor (Author's coll.). Bottom: a "Panther" tank abandoned on the Vimoutiers-Chambois road (IWM). Opposite page: wrecked German vehicles seen from an Allied reconnaissance plane at the end of August 1944 (IWM).*

bat Groups each under the command of tough officers. He would send them to attack the slopes with a tank or a self propelled gun as they came out of the corridor.

All the units still in the trap from the woods of Gouffern to the River Dives knew well that now the only road to freedom was the corridor opened by Meindl, first the bridges and then the hillsides.

All day long the eastern part of Saint-Lambert with its bridges and the crossroads remained in German hands but under constant shelling of the Canadian artillery one mile away.

At noon, the 10th SS-Panzerdivision and the 116th Panzerdivision forming the group "Army Command" cleared the bridges and kept them to allow the General Headquarters and its commanding General, General Hausser to go by. Clinging to a tank like an infantryman General Hausser crossed the river and was once again wounded in the face. He had already lost an eye in Russia.

Then what was left of the infantrymen of the 12th SS-Panzerdivision "Hitlerjugend", 400 men determined to pass, suddenly turned up on the main road of Saint-Lambert and at the sound of a whistle jumped on a Canadian patrol, disarmed the men and abandoned them on the spot. The Germans vanished as fast as they had come.

The 116th Panzerdivision coming from Tournai with 8 vehicles abreast on the road arrived at the bridges at Saint-Lambert, cleared them of the obstructions caused by Allied artillery relentlessly pounding the approaches. Canadian tanks were engaged near the crossroads but the Germans managed to hold the bridges all day long. Tanks, guns, track vehicles rushing to force the passage, attacked the Canadians who put up some opposition and then took the road to the hills where things were easier.

From the belfry of the church of Saint-Lambert, General von Luttwitz, who commanded the 2nd Panzerdivision, and General Straube, the commander of the 47th Armd.Corps, were directing the traffic at the bridge and the crossroads. "It was a particularly terrifying affair, men, horses, vehicles and lots of stores were hit while trying to cross over and had been pushed into the ravine of the River Dives to clear the way and they piled up in horrible looking masses of debris.. In a narrow street, a group of motorcycle riders had been knocked out, their machines were still burning with their riders completely charred on their seats. At the crossroads, against the wall of a house, a pile of mutilated and dismembered corpses had been run over by a Panther tank. During the whole afternoon, some Sherman tanks tried to enter Saint-Lambert unsuceesfully. They were repelled by our own tanks and anti-tank guns which kept the corridor Saint-Lambert/Coudehard open."

Von Luttwitz decided to leave the bridge at 9 p.m. after forming combat groups and ordering then to walk northeast. He met Meindl at midnight, helped him at his HQ of La Cour-du-Bocq, and then reached Vimoutiers.

Major Currie reported that he had destroyed a "Panzer IV" and an 88 mm gun at the crossroads and then sent a hundred artillery salvoes on the houses of the crossroads where the Germans were assembled, which dissuaded the Germans from attacking. But the fantastic traffic over the bridge could not be stopped that day. It was like a valve through which the whole pocket was deflated.

At 10.30 p.m. the Canadians reached the bridges but they were repelled once more by determined German troops coming from farther away. 900 men of the 227th Inf.Div. crossed at Saint-Lambert under artillery fire. Some elements of the 326th Inf.Div. preferred dumping some vehicles in the river in order to cross over them. It was a general stampede, there were cries, insults, threats and all that under a deluge of shells which fell on this human misery and added to the suffering of the horses driven mad and entangled in their harnesses who were hit and wounded trying to escape. During the night, an infantry regiment with 50 vehicles and 5 guns of the 116th Pz.Div. got lost and was captured at Magny together with 20 armoured vehicles and 80 elements of the Engineers. Some had escaped before them, but few were going to follow them.

The German report of Army Group B for the day mentioned: "At daybreak, the 7th Army, the 2nd Parachute Corps and the 47th Armd. Corps leading the way, followed by the 74th and 84th Corps attempted to cross the lines towards the north-east. The first attack failed. But after an attack of the 3rd Parachute Division, it was possible to break through at Saint-Lambert and then make the gap wide enough for the 74th and the 84th Corps to try to escape. Most vehicles, guns an heavy weapons had to be abandoned for two reasons: the air attacks and the lack of petrol. It took five hours of fighting at Saint-Lambert to break through. Without any radio communications, the Army could no longer transmit orders. Nevertheless the conduct of the troops who managed to escape was wonderful."

*A "Strumgeschütz IV" destroyed between Ronai and Nécy. The picture was taken a year after the end of the fighting (author's coll.).*

## b) The Polish bulwark of "Maczuga". August 20.

When the mist cleared up on Sunday morning, the Poles could not believe what they could see below them. All the valley, all the slopes were congested with long columns advancing along the lanes and across the orchards towards them. They were mown down by the Polish artillery. This assault of the paratroopers and SS soldiers on the hillsides of Coudehard was followed by 8 more during the day, each time they were repelled with frightful losses, the last one being launched at 7.30 p.m.

On the other side of "Maczuga", the tanks of the 2nd SS Armd. Corps engaged the Polish armour from a long way off and outclassed them by the quality of their armament. This hindered the junction of the squadrons of the 4th Canadian Armd.Div. with the 1st and 2nd Polish regiments which had been encircled and were short of ammunition. The infantry of "Das Reich", supported by the salvoes of heavy electric mortars, charged the northern slopes and was repelled.

Those who had attacked at Coudehard managed to create a gap at Boisjos and the German portable anti-tank weapons played havoc with Polish vehicles. Those who were fleeing managed to cross the Polish lines and to infiltrate the neighbourhood because of their great numbers. Losses were terrific, as men resorted to bayonets and knives. As soon as a sector had been cleared, German light vehicles would rush into it and reach the Champosoult-Vimoutiers road. While some were fighting, others were organizing the escape of equipment through the gaps of Cour du Boscq and Boisjos. On the slopes of the hill, corpses were piling up and the Poles were soon protected by a human rampart.

On road D 16, a battalion of infantry of "Das Reich" coming from the north helped a combat group coming out of the pocket and maintained the gap open until 7 p.m. between the 2 ends of the club.

At about 7 p.m. at Coudehard, Meindl obtained a truce from the Poles and the Canadians for 20 minutes to evacuate the casualties in open ambulances driving in a convoy under the Allied guns which remained silent. Then shelling was resumed and the rush towards "Meindl Crossroads" continued as before.

At 7.30 p.m. a last assault of the SS-grenadiers against the northern slope of Hill 262 impressed the Poles so much that they stopped shooting for a while at those young men who sang "Deutschland über Alles" at the top of their voices and then fell to the last bullets of the Poles who had but 50 rounds left each and 5 shells per gun. The light weapons which could not longer be used could be easily replaced by thoses found on the ground. On road D 16, at the same moment, 2000 fleeing Germans took advantage of the fact that the Poles were busy further north, to pass with armoured vehicles between the gutted wrecks of tanks and trucks.

At nightfall only 4 sound officers out of 60 were left on "Maczuga" and 110 men able to fight out of an initial 1500. At midnight it started raining, a blessing for thousands of men that Meindl was watching trying to escape. Then the human flood dwindled to a trickle and then nothing. At dawn on August 21 an armoured detachment of the rear guard signalled "nothing behind". Meindl halted two vehicles, woke his companions up and climbed on board. It was 5 a.m.

## Monday August 21.

It was raining. At Mont-Ormel, near road D.16 the last suicidal attacks began in the morning on the southeastern slope. As usual they were decimated by the fire of the Polish automatic weapon. The last attack started from the Chapel at Coudehard and was repelled with 50% losses for the Germans.

At midday the "Canadian Grenadier Guards" had fought their way to the small wood of Cour-du-Bosq. There they saw exhausted soldiers running towards them, crying for joy and relief. Their siege had been lifted ; wounded soldiers and prisoners were evacuated and supplies could now reach them.

The 9th SS-Panzerdivision on the road to Champosoult also reported that only small groups were now coming from time to time having no knowledge of what was going on elsewhere.

At Saint-Lambert the fighting at the river crossings lessened considerably by midday. The village was on fire. The Canadians were now fighting around the bridges. Two half track vehicles carrying white flags offered the surrender of 800 men some fit, some wounded. Stragglers were also caught at the bridges as late as 4.30 p.m. The 3rd Canadian Inf.Div. came to relieve the Currie Group which left the wrecks of 9 Sherman tanks and 12 self-propelled anti-tank guns on the ground, but 7 German tanks had been destroyed, 300 Germans killed, 500 wounded and 2100 taken prisoner.

At Tournai the bombardment by Allied artillery ceased only when 2700 Germans who were not willing to fight any longer left the village to reach Chambois in an orderly fashion.

At 4.30 p.m. General Bittrich ordered his 2nd SS-Armd.Corps to wtihdraw towards Orbec: its costly mission had been accomplished. A unit of paratroopers greatly impressed his men in marching in quick time out of "cauldron" and singing as they went.

### Tuesday August 22nd.

At 4 a.m. the Canadians of the 3rd Inf.Div. entered Tournai. Here they gathered 150 more prisoners who were not so eager to surrender. The 80th US Inf.Div. coming from Aubry-en-Exmes

*Between Ronai and Nécy, after the battle (author's coll.).*

which had been liberated in the morning, met them in that place at 8 a.m. The artillery became silent after firing 15,000 shells in 4 days at that little town.
On Tuesday morning at 8 a.m. *the battle of Normandy was over.*

### THE AFTERMATH OF THE BATTLE OF THE POCKET / AN EVALUATION.

As of August 25th, the complement of the 5th Panzerarmee rescued from the pocket was 17,980 men - the equivalent of the normal complement of one division -, 314 guns, 72 tanks and assault guns. This consisted of the following:
- 2nd Panzerdivision: 0 tank, 0 gun, 1 infantry battalion.
- 21st Panzerdivision: 10 tanks, O gun, 4 infantry battalions.
- 116th Panzerdivision: 12 tanks, 2 batteries, 1 inf.battalion.
- Panzer-Lehr: 0 tank, 0 gun, 190 men.
- 1st SS-Pz Div. "Liebstandarte Adolf Hitler": O tank, 0 gun, 300 men.
- 2nd SS-Panzerdivision "Das Reich": 15 tanks, 6 guns, 450 grenadiers.
- 9th SS-Panzerdivision "Hohenstaufen": 25 tanks, 20 guns, 460 grenadiers.
- 10th SS-Panzerdivision "Frundsberg": 0 tank, 0 gun, 4 undermanned inf. battalions.
- 12th SS-Panzerdivision "Hitlerjugend": 10 tanks, 0 gun, 300 men (infantry). This armoured unit had a total of 20,000 men on June 1 and was equipped with 139 operational tanks.
On the Allied side:
- the 1st Polish Armd.Div.: 325 men killed, 1,002 wounded, 114 missing, that is 20% of its combat strenght.
- The Canadian 4th Armd.Div. and 3rd Inf.Div.: 260 losses.
- The 90th US Inf.Div. and 80th US Inf.Div. 760 casualties for the same period from Argentan to Chambois.
One must also mention 82 civilian victims.

Finally, 10,000 Germans were put out of action in 4 days and 40,000 were captured, but as many, that is about 50,000 managed to escape after abandonning their equipment.
On August 23 Eisenhower visited the area. He said later that while walking there he had discovered a scene that only Dante could have described. For hundreds of metres one could walk only on decaying human remains, in ominous silence, in luxuriant countryside which life had suddenly deserted to be replaced by destruction and death. He could tread on hundreds of rifles scattered along the muddy lanes and see hundreds more piled up along sheds. For a mile vehicles had been strafed and burnt, some had been fused together.
Three hundred vehicles had been trapped on that road by planes and then despatched by artillery fire, some of them were hemmed in but still intact. There were no foxholes nor shelters of any description, too much in a hurry or too tired, the Germans had not bothered digging in, too exhausted even to surrender."
It was in this bocage that the outcome of the Battle of France was decided: reeling after 77 days of a war of attrition the Wehrmacht received its final blow there. 12 days later Monty entered Antwerp.
A deathlike silence had fallen on the valley and its hillsides. They would not receive medical clearance for four months. After that apocalypse, life deserted the desolated area between Saint-Lambert and Chambois for weeks.

### DRIVING THROUGH THE POCKET

One can leave Argentan which was captured by the infantry of the 80th US Inf.Div. and take the Argentan-Vimoutiers road N 816. That road was crossed by 100,000 Germans and their vehicles towards the hills of Auge between August 17 and 20. That road formed the western boundary of the pocket and was constantly watched over by Allied planes and artillery. At the exit of Forêt de Gouffern one can see the whole panorama of this sector eastwards.Bailleul and Villedieu were captured by the 53rd Welsh Division on August 20. Trun was the north-western end of the pocket. Turn right at the main crossroads of the town and take the road D 13 going towards the centre of the pocket, towards Chambois. One can notice that the houses of Saint-Lambert have not much changed if one compares them with the photos taken by the Canadians on August 19, 1944 at this very spot. The "Death Corridor" between Saint-Lambert and the hamlet of Moissy stretches to the left towards the hills. One can reach it by following the road D 16 in the direction of Vimoutiers. On the main square of Chambois a panel mentions the closing of the pocket and the end of the Battle of Normandy.

5 kilometres further north, at Mont-Ormel one can have a wonderful view from the monument which was erected in 1965 and dedicated by General Maczek in the presence of General Langlade, Colonel Zgorzelski and Captain Waters of the US Army who effected their historical link in Chambois on August 19. The monument is situated on Hill 262, "Maczuga" where, from August 18 to 22, 1944, according to their leader "each soldier sacrificed everything for the sake of liberty". To the west one can see the valley of the River Dives which was the grave of the 7th German Army.

The road D 16 going to Vimoutiers was one of the most difficult for the Germans to use to escape from the trap for it was under direct view of the Poles

*The corpse of this German soldier was found 15 years after the war. (author's coll.).*

established on "Maczuga" and well known to Allied fighter-bombers. At Vimoutiers one can see a German "Tiger" tank of the 2nd SS-Armoured Corps which had remained in a ditch for thirty years and was placed there in 1976 on the road to Gacé.

---

**Some figures**

- Between June 6 and August 25, 1944, 2 million allied soldiers (1.2 million Americans and others attached to the US Army, and 800,000 British and Canadians) landed on the Normandy beaches or the Mulberry Harbour of Arromanches.
- 740,000 German soldiers opposed them.
- The Allies lost 206,703 men in Normandy (124,394 Americans and 82,309 British and Canadians).
- The Germans had 240,000 losses and 210,000 prisoners. They also abandoned 80% of their stores on the battlefield.
- The Départements of La Manche and Calvados were devastated and the civil population suffered 45,000 casualties, including 10,000 killed.
- The beautiful Norman countryside was strewn with mines, most of the cattle had been slaughtered and the meadows were full of craters, the trees had lost their leaves and branches and no bird sang. After the armies had passed, life seemed to have been replaced by destruction, silence and death.

---

*The memorial museum of Bayeux (Photo Vincent Cazin-Ville de Bayeux).*

## Organigramme de la 2ème Division blindée française
## (rattachée au XVème corps expéditionnaire US)

| Blindés | Quartier Général |
|---|---|
| 501ème Régt de chars de combat (501 R.C.C.)<br>12ème Régt de cuirassiers (12ème R.C.)<br>12ème Régt de Chasseurs d'Afrique (12e R.C.A)<br>Régt blindé de Fusiliers Marins (R.B.F.M.) | Groupement de reconn.<br>1er Régt de Marche de<br>Spahis marocains<br>(1er R.M.S.M.) |
| Infanterie | Génie |
| Régiment de Marche du Tchad | 13e Bat.Génie(I3°BG) |
| Artillerie | Transmissions |
| 1er groupe du 3ème régiment d'artillerie<br>coloniale(1 / 3° RRC)<br><br>1er groupe du 40ème régiment d'artillerie<br>nord-africain (1 / 40 RANA)<br>11ème groupe du 64ème régiment d'artill.<br>de D.B. (XI° / 64° RADB)<br>22ème groupe colonial de forces terrestres<br>antiaériennes (22° FTA) | 97° / 84° compagnie mixte<br>de transmissions<br>(97° / 84° CMT)<br><br><br>Train<br>97ème cie de Q.G.<br>197°&297° cies de transport<br>397° cie de circulation route.<br>497 cie de services |
| Santé : 13ème bataillon médical. | |

# UNITES BRITANNIQUES DANS LA BATAILLE DE NORMANDIE

## Organigramme de la 3ème DI (3rd Inf.Div.)

| 8th Brigade | 9th Brigade | 185th Brigade |
|---|---|---|
| 1st Suffolk Regt<br>2nd East<br>Yorkshire Regt<br>1st South<br>Lancashire Regt. | 2nd Lincolnshire Regt<br>1st K.O.S.B. Regt<br><br>2nd R.U.R. Regt | 2R[al]Warwickshire Regt<br>1st Royal Norfolk Regt<br><br>2nd K.S.L.I. Regt |
| Royal Artillery | Rég. de reconnaissance | Bat. de mitrailleuses |
| 7th, 33rd, 76th Field R.<br>20th A.T. Regt<br>92nd LAA Regt | 3rd Recce Regt RAC<br>(Northumberland Fus.) | 2nd (M.G) Middlesex Regt. |

## Organigramme de la 15th (Scottish) Division

| 44th (Lowland)Brigade | 46th (Highland) Brigade | 227th (Highland) Brig. |
|---|---|---|
| 8th Royal Scots<br>6th Royal Scots Fusil.<br>6th K.O.S.B. | 9th Cameronians<br>2nd Glasgow Highlanders<br>7th Seaforth Highlanders | 10 th Highland Light Infant.<br>2nd Gordon Highlanders<br>2nd Argyll and<br>Sutherland Highlanders |
| Royal Artillery | Régt. de reconnaissance | Bat. de mitrailleuses |
| 131st,181st,190thField<br>Regts R.A.<br>97th A.T. Regt, R.A. | 15th Recce Regt RAC | 1st (M.G.) Middlesex<br>Regt |

## Organigramme de la 43rd (Wessex) Division

| 129th Brigade | 130th Brigade | 214th Brigade |
|---|---|---|
| 4th Somerset Light<br>Infantry<br>4th & 5th Wiltshire Reg | 7th Hampshire Regt<br>4th and 5th Dorsetshire<br>Regt. | 7th Somerset L.I.<br>1st Worcestershire Regt<br>5th Duke of Cornwall's<br>Light Infantry |
| Royal Artillery | Régt de reconnaissance | Bat. de mitrailleuses |
| 94th,112th,179th Field<br>Artillery Regts,R.A.<br>59th A.T. Regt, R.A. | 43rd Recce<br>(Gloucestershire)<br>Regt.,R.A.C. | 8th Middlesex Regt |

## Organigramme de la 49th (West Riding) Division

| 70th Brigade | 146th Brigade | 147th Brigade |
|---|---|---|
| 10th and 11th Durham<br>Light Infantry<br>1st Tyneside Scottish | 4th Lincol Regt<br>1 / 4th King'Own Yorkshire<br>Light Infantry<br>Hallamshire Battalion<br>The York and Lancaster<br>Regt | 11th Royal Scots Fusiliers<br>6th Duke of Wellington's<br>Regt (to 6/7/44)<br>1st Leicestershire Regt<br>(from 6/7/44)<br>7th Duke of Wellington's<br>Regt |
| Royal Artillery | Régt de reconnaissance | Bat. de mitrailleuses |
| 69th,143rd,185th Field<br>Artillery Regts,R.A.<br>55th A.T. Regt, R.A. | 49th Recce Regt, R.A.C. | 2nd Princesse Louise's<br>Kensington Regt (M.G.) |

## Organigramme de la 50th (Northumbrian) Division

| 69th Brigade | 151th Brigade | 231st Brigade |
|---|---|---|
| 5th East Yorkshire Regt<br>6th Green Howards<br>7th Green Howards | 6th Durham L.I.<br>9th Durham L.I.<br>8th Durham L.I. | 2nd Devonshire Regt<br>1st Hampshire Regt<br>1st Dorsetshire Regt |
| Royal Artillery | Régt de reconnaissance | Bat. de mitrailleuses |
| 74th, 90th, 124th, Field<br>Artillery A.T. Regt, R.A.<br>102nd A.T. Regt,R.A. | 61st Recce Regt R.A.C. | 2nd Cheshire Regt (M.G.) |

## Organigramme de la 51st (highland) Division

| 152nd Brigade | 153rd Brigade | 154rd Brigade |
|---|---|---|
| 2nd Seaforth Highlanders<br>5th Seaforth Highlanders<br>5th Q.O.Cameron<br>Highlanders | 5th Black Watch<br>1st Gordon Highlanders<br>5th/7th Gordon Highl. | 1st Black Watch<br>7th Black Watch<br>7th Argyll and Sutherland<br>Highlanders |
| Royal Artillery | Régt de reconnaissance | Bat. de mitrailleuses |
| 126th, 127th, 128th Field<br>Artillery Regts, R.A.<br>61st A.T. Regt, R.A. | 2nd Derbyshire Yeomanry,<br>R.A.C. | 1/7th Middlesex Regt<br>(M.G.) |

## Organigramme de la 53rd (Welsh) Division

| 71st Brigade | 158th Brigade | 160th Brigade |
|---|---|---|
| 1st East Lancashire Regt<br>(to 3/8/44)<br>1st Ox and Bucks L.I.<br>1st Highland L.I.<br>4th Royal Welsh<br>Fusiliers | 4th & 6th Royal Welsh<br>Fusiliers (to 3/8/44)<br>1/5th The Welsh Regt<br>(from 4/8/44)<br>7th Royal Welsh Fus.<br>1st East Lancashire Regt<br>(from 4/8/44) | 2nd Monmouthshire Regt<br>4th The Welsh Regt<br>1/5th The Welsh Regt<br>6th The Royal Welsh<br>Fusiliers |
| Royal Artillery | Régt de reconnaissance | Bat. de mitrailleuses |
| 81st, 83rd, 133rd Field<br>Artillery Regts, R.A.<br>71st A.T. Regt. | 53 Recce Regt, R.A.C. | 1st Manchester Regt (M.G.). |

## Organigramme de la 59ème (Staffordshire) Division

| 176th Brigade | 177th Brigade | 197th Brigade |
|---|---|---|
| 7th Royal Norfolk Regt<br>7th Sth Staffordshire Rg.<br>6th Nth Staffordshire Rg. | 5th South Staff. Regt<br>1/6th South Staff.<br>2/6th South Staff. | 1/7th Royal Warwickshire<br>Fusiliers<br>2/5th The Lancashire<br>Fusiliers<br>5th East Lancashire Regt |
| Royal Artillery | Regt de reconnaissance | Bat. de mitrailleuses |
| 61st, 110th, 116th Field<br>Artillery Regts, R.A.<br>68th A.T. Regt, R.A. | 59th Recce Regt, R.A.C. | 7th Royal Northumberland<br>Fusiliers (M.G.) |

## Organigramme de la Division Blindée de la Garde (Guards Arm. Div.)

| 5ème Brig. blindée de la Garde | 32ème Brig. d'inf. de la Garde (32nd Guards Brigade) | |
|---|---|---|
| 2nd (Arm.) Btlion Grenadier Guards<br>1st (Arm.) Btlion Coldstream Guards<br>2nd (Arm.) Btlion Irish Guards | 5th Btlion Coldstream Guards<br>3rd Blion Irish Guards<br>1st Btlion Welsh Guards | |
| Royal Artillery | Régt de Reconnaissance | Cie de mitrailleuses |
| 55th, 153th (Lanc.Yeo.)<br>F.A. Regts<br>21st A.T. Regt<br>94th LAA Regt | Welsh Guards (2nd Arm. Recce Btlion) | (3rd Ind. M.G. Coy)<br>Royal Northumberland Fusiliers |
| | Motor Btlion : 1 (Motor) Btlion Grenadier Guards. | |

## Organigramme de la 7ème Division blindée (7th Arm.Div.)

| 22ème Brig. blindée | 131ème Brig. d'inf. | Motor Batalion |
|---|---|---|
| 4th County of London Yeo (Sharpshooters)<br>1st Royal Tank Regt<br>5th Royal Tank Regt | 1/5th Queen's 1st Btl<br>1/6th Queen's<br>1/7th Queen's | 1st Btn<br>The Rifle Brigade |
| Royal Artillery | Régt de Reconnaissance | Cie de mitrailleuses |
| 3rd, 5th Royal Horse Artillery.<br>65th A.T. Regt<br>15th LAA Regt | 8th King's Royal Hussars (Arm. recce Regt) | Royal Northumberland Fusiliers |

## Organigramme de la 11ème Division Blindée (11th Arm. Div.)

| 29ème Brig.blindée<br>23rd Hussars<br>2nd Fife and Forfar Yeo.<br>3rd Royal Tank Regt | 159ème Brig. d'inf.<br>3rd Monmouth<br>4th KSLI<br>1st Herefords | Motor Batalion<br>8th (Motor Btn)<br>The Rifle Brigade |
|---|---|---|
| Royal Artillery | Régt de reconnaissance | Cie de Mitrailleuses |
| 151st (Ayrshire Yeo)<br>13th Royal Horse Arty.<br>75th (Norfolk Yeo) A.T. R<br>58th LAA Regt | 2nd Northants Yeo.<br>(Arm. Recce Regt) | Royal Northumberland Fusiliers |

## Organigramme de la 79ème Division Blindée (79th Arm. Div.)

| 1ère Tank Brigade | 30ème Brig. blindée | 1st Assault Brigade R.E |
|---|---|---|
| 11th R.T.R. (S.W.B.)<br>42nd R.T.R.(23rd London Regt.)<br>49th R.T.R | 22nd Dragoons<br>1st Lothian and Border Horse<br>2nd C.L.Y. (Westminster Dragoons)<br>141st R.A.C. (The Buffs) | 5th Assault Regt, R.E.<br>6th Assault Regt, R.E.<br>42nd Assault Regt,R.E. |

## Organigramme de la 6ème Division Aéroportée britannique

| 3rd Parachute Brigade | 5th Parachute Brigade |
|---|---|
| 8th Btlion The Parachute Regt<br>9th Btlion The Parachute Regt<br>1st Canadian Parachute Btlion | 22nd Parachute Independant Company<br>7th Btlion The Parachute Regt<br>12th Btlion The Para. Regt (Green Howards)<br>13th Btlion The Para.Regt (2/4th South Lancs) |
| 6th Airlanding Brigade | Divisional Troops |
| 12th Devonshire Regt<br>2nd Ox and Bucks L.I.<br>1st Royal Ulster Rifles | 6th Airborne Arm.Recce Regt. R.A.C.<br>53rd (Worcestershire Hussars) Airlanding A.T. Regt, R.A.<br>6th Airborne Div.Engineers<br>6th Airborne Div.Signals |

**1ère Brigade Belge d'infanterie**

| |
|---|
| 1ère, 2ème et 3ème unités motorisées - batterie d'artillerie<br>escadron d'autos blindées - compagnie du génie - brigade train |

**Organigramme de la 56ème Brigade d'infanterie indépendante brit.**

| |
|---|
| 2nd South Wales Borderers - 2nd Gloucestershire Regt - 2nd Essex Regt |

## Organigramme de la 2ème Brigade blindée canadienne<br>(2nd Canadian Armoured Brigade)

| |
|---|
| 6ème Régt Blindé (Ist Hussars)<br>10ème Régt blindé (Fort Garry Horse)<br>27ème Régt blindé (Sherbrooke Fusiliers Regt)<br>H.Q. defence platoon (7th/11th R.C.H.) |

## Organigramme de la 31ème Brigade indépendante de chars britannique

| |
|---|
| 7th R.T.R.jusqu'au 17/8/44<br>9th R.T.R. jusqu'au 31/8/44<br>144th R.A.C. (8th East Lancashire) 23-31/8/44 |

## Organigramme de la 1ère Division blindée polonaise

| 10ème Brigade blindée | 3ème Brigade de chasseurs |
|---|---|
| 1er Régt blindé<br>2ème Régt blindé<br>24ème Lanciers<br>10ème Dragons (portés) | 1er bataillon de chasseurs de Podhale<br>8ème Bataillon de chasseurs<br>9ème Bataillon de chasseurs<br>M.G. Bataillon (mitrailleuses) |
| Artillerie | Régiment de Reconnaissance |
| 1er et 2ème Régiments<br>d'artillerie motorisée | 10ème Chasseurs à cheval |
| 1er Régiment antichars<br>1er Régiment antiaérien | Services<br>Effectifs : 855 officiers, 15.210 hommes,<br>    4431 véhicules dont 381 chars,<br>    473 pièces d'artillerie |

**Organigramme de la 34ème Brigade indépendante de chars brit.**

107th R.A.C. (5th K.O. Royal Regt) - 147th R.A.C. (10th Hampshire Regt)
153rd R.A.C. (8th Essex Regt) jusqu'au 24/8/44.

**Organigramme de la 6ème Brigade indépendante de chars brit.**

4th Tank Btlion Grenadier Guards - 4th Tank Btlion Coldstream Guards
3rd Tank Btlion Scots Guards

**Organigramme de la 27ème Brigade blindée indépendante brit.**

13th/18th Royal Hussars - 1st East Riding Yeomanry -
The Staffordshire Yeomanry.

**Organigramme de la 33ème Brigade indépendante de chars brit.**

1st Northamptonshire Yeomanry -144th R.A.C. (8th East Lancs.) jusqu'au 22/8/44
148th R.A.C. (9th Loyal Regt) jusqu'au 16/8/44 - 1st East Riding Yeomanry, depuis le 16 août.

**Organigramme des commandos de l'armée et de la marine brit.**

1st Special Briqgade (1st S.S. Bde)
N°3 Cdo/N° 4 Cdo, plus 2 "Free-French" troops N 10 (Inter-Allied) Cdo/
N°6 Cdo/45 Royal Marine Cdo/2nd Royal Marine Arm. Support Regt/
5th Ind. R.M.Aed Support Btty/R.M. Engineer Cdo (1 troop).

**4th Special Service Brigade (4th S.S.Bde)**

41 Royal Marine Cdo/46 Royal Marine Cdo/47 Royal Marine Cdo
48 Royal Marine Cdo/1st Royal Marine Arm. Support Regt/R.M. Engineer Cdo

**Organigramme de la 4ème Brigade blindée indépendante brit.**

The Royal Scots Greys - 3rd C.L.Y.(Sharpshooters) jusqu'au 28.7.44
3rd/4th C.L.Y. (Sharpshooters) depuis le 29.7.44 - 44th R.T.R.
2nd K.R.R.C. infanterie motorisée

**Organigramme de la 8ème Brigade blindée indépendante brit.**

4th/7th Royal Dragoon Guards - 24th Lancers jusqu'au 29/7/44
The Nottinghamshire Yeomanry - 13th/18th Hussars depuis le 29/7/44
12th K.R.R.C. (2nd Queens Westminster) infanterie motorisée.

**Organigramme de la 2ème Division d'Infanterie canadienne**

| 4ème Brigade d'Inf. | 5ème Brigade d'Inf. |
|---|---|
| The Royal Regt of Canada | The Black Watch (Royal Highland Regt) of Canada |
| The Royal Hamilton L.I. | Le Régiment de Maisonneuve |
| The Essex Scottish Regt | The Calgary Highlanders |

| 6ème Brigade d'Inf. | Régiment de reconnaissance |
|---|---|
| Les Fusiliers Mont-Royal | 8ème Régt de recc. 14th Canadian Hussars) |
| The Queen's Own Cameron | |
| Highlanders of Canada | Mitrailleuses |
| The Sth Saskatchewan Regt | The Toronto Scottish Regt |

| Artillerie divisionnaire |
|---|
| 4ème, 5ème, 6ème Régts de campagne ; 2ème Régt antichars |

## Organigramme de la 3ème Division d'Infanterie canadienne

| 7ème Brigade d'Inf. | 8ème Brigade d'Inf. |
|---|---|
| The Royal Winnipeg Rifles<br>The Regina Rifles<br>1stBtn,The Canadian Scot.R | The Queen's Own Rifles of Canada<br>Le Régiment de la Chaudière<br>The North Shore (New Brunswick) Regt |
| 9ème Brigade d'Inf. | Régiment de Reconnaissance |
| The Highland L.I. of Canada<br>The Stormont, Dundas<br>and Glengarry Highlanders<br>The North Nova Scotia<br>Highlanders | 7ème Régt (17th Duke of York's R.C.H.)<br>Mitrailleuses<br><br>The Cameron Highlanders of Canada |
| Artillerie divisionnaire | |
| 12ème, 13ème, 14ème Régts de campagne ; 3ème Régt antichars | |

## Organigramme de la 4ème Division Blindée canadienne

| 4ème Brigade blindée | 10ème Brigade d'Infanterie |
|---|---|
| 21ème Régt blindé<br>(The Governor General's<br>Foot Guards)<br>22ème Régt blindé<br>(The Canadian Grenadier<br>Guards)<br>28ème Régt blindé<br>(The British Columbia Regt) | The Lincoln and Welland Regt<br>The Algonquin Regt<br>The Argyll and Sutherland Highlanders<br>of Canada<br>The Lake Superior Regt(motorisé) |
| Artillerie divisionnaire | Régiment de Reconnaissance |
| 15ème Régt de campagne<br>23ème Régt de campagne<br>(automoteur)<br>5ème Régt antichars | 29ème (The South Alberta Regt)<br>Mitrailleuses<br>10ème Cie ind. de mitrailleuses<br>(The New Brunswick Rangers). |

## Troupes de la 1ère Armée canadienne

| |
|---|
| 25ème Régt blindé de remplacements (The Elgin Regt)<br>1er Régt blindé de transports de troupes (Kangaroos)<br>Artillerie Royale canadienne :<br>     -11ème Régt de campagne<br>     -1er, 2ème, 5ème Régts d'artillerie moyenne<br>Génie, Transmissions, Santé, Mécanique...<br>Bat. de défense du QG de la 1ère Armée (Royal Montreal Regt).<br><br>18ème Régt blindé (12th Manitoba Dragoons)<br>6ème Régiment antichars<br>Génie, Transmissions, Santé, Parc, Mécanique, Prévoté...<br>Compagnie de défense du IIème Corps (The Prince Edward Island Light Horse) |

# UNITES AMERICAINES DANS LA BATAILLE DE NORMANDIE

## Organigramme des divisions d'infanterie US
## US. Inf. Div. Order of battle

| | Régts d'inf.<br>Inf. Regts | Bataillons d'artillerie<br>Arty. Btlions | Bat. Génie<br>Engineers | Bat.Santé<br>Medics |
|---|---|---|---|---|
| 1ère DI | 16ème, 18°, 26° | 5°, 7°, 32°, 33° | 1° | 1° |
| 2ème DI | 9°, 23°, 38° | 12°, 15°, 37°, 38° | 2° | 2° |
| 4ème DI | 8°, 12°, 22° | 20°, 9°, 42°, 44° | 4° | 4° |
| 5ème DI | 2°, 10°, 11° | 19°, 21°, 46°, 50° | 7° | 5° |
| 8ème DI | 13°, 28°, 121° | 28°, 43°, 45°, 56° | 12° | 8° |
| 9ème DI | 39°, 47°, 60°, | 26°, 34°, 60°, 84° | 15°9° | |
| 28ème DI | 9°, 109°, 110°, 112° | 101°, 108°, 109°, 229°103° | 103° | |
| 29ème DI | 115°, 116°, 175° | 110°, 111°, 224°, 227° | 121° | 104° |
| 30ème DI | 117°, 119°, 120° | 113°, 118°, 197°, 230° | 105° | 105° |
| 35ème DI | 134°, 137°, 320° | 127°, 161°, 216°, 219° | 60 | 110° |
| 79ème DI | 313°, 318°, 319° | 313°, 314°, 315°, 905° | 305° | 305° |
| 83ème DI | 329°, 330°, 331° | 322°, 323°, 324°, 908° | 308° | 308° |
| 90ème DI | 357°, 358°, 359° | 343°, 344°, 345°, 915° | 315° | 315° |

## Organigramme des divisions blindées US
## US Armored Dlv. Order of Battle

| | Esc.de Recon<br>Cavalry Rec.<br>Squadron | Bat. de chars<br>Tank Batalions | Bat.inf.<br>blindée<br>Arm.Inf.Btlins | Bat.d'art.<br>blindée<br>Arm.Fld.Ary.B |
|---|---|---|---|---|
| 2ème DB | 82° | 41°, 63°, 67° | | 14°, 78°, 92° |
| 3ème DB | 83° | 32°, 33°, 36° | | 54°, 67°, 391° |
| 4ème DB | 25° | 10°, 51°, 53° | 8°, 35°, 37° | 22°, 66°, 94° |
| 5ème DB | 85° | 15°,46°, 47° | 10°, 34°, 81°, | 47°, 71°, 95° |
| 6ème DB | 86° | 9°, 44°, 50° | 15°, 68°, 69° | 128°,212°,231° |

## Organigramme des formations aéroportées US
## US Airborne Formations "Order of Battle"

| | Régts d'Inf.Para.<br>Parachute Inf.<br>Regts. | Régts d'Inf.<br>Glider Inf.<br>Regts | Bat.art.para<br>Para F.A<br>Btlions | Bat.art.plané<br>Glider<br>F.A. Bt. | Génie aérop.<br>Airborne<br>Engineers |
|---|---|---|---|---|---|
| 82°D.A.<br>Airborne | 505°, 507°, 508° | 325 / 401° | 456° | 319°, 320° | 307° |
| 101° D.A. | 501°, 502°, 506°, | 327 / 401° | 377° | 321°, 907° | 326° |

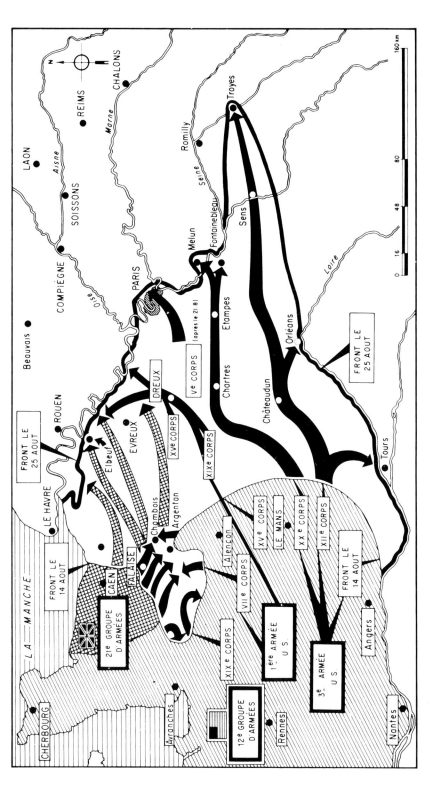

**Évolution de la situation du 14 au 25 août.** Les opérations de fermeture de la Poche de Falaise se déroulent du 16 au 20 août puis le XV$^e$ corps oblique vers la Seine pour tenter de couper la retraite aux Allemands. Ce corps d'armée est alors rattaché à la 1$^{re}$ Armée tandis que la 3$^e$ Armée fonce vers l'est pour atteindre la Lorraine, puis l'Allemagne. Mais elle sera d'abord bloquée sur la Moselle et s'enlisera dans la boue en Lorraine (carte Heimdal).

# Par Georges BERNAGE

Dans son étude (art. cité p. 114), Michel Dufresne a fait un remarquable décompte des 44 800 Allemands qui sont sortis de la Poche. Nous reprenons ici certains chiffres en ordre décroissant ; On verra que les divisions blindées ont sorti plus d'hommes que les divisions d'infanterie : 10 000 hommes pour la *1. SS-Panzer-Division*, 10 000 hommes pour la *10. SS-Panzer-Division*, 8 000 hommes pour la *2. Panzer-Division*, 5 000 hommes pour la *3. Fallschirmjäger-Division* (parachutistes), 2 000 hommes pour la *276. Infanterie-Division*, la *277. Infanterie-Division*, la *353. Infanterie-Division*. Les *84. ID, 326. ID, 363. ID* ramènent chacune 1 000 hommes. Trois divisions blindées font sortir des effectifs faibles : 1 000 hommes pour la *9. Panzer-Division*, 500 hommes pour la *12. SS-Panzer-Division*, et 300 hommes pour la *116. Panzer-Division*. Mais en fait, ces trois divisions n'avaient laissé dans la Poche de Falaise que des groupements tactiques (des *Kampfgruppen*). La *12. SS-Panzer-Division* a rassemblé 11 500 hommes près de Verneuil-sur-Avre. Ainsi, cette division dispose encore d'un total de 12 000 hommes mais seulement de 10 chars. Dans son historique de la division (*Kriegsgeschichte der 12. SS-Panzer-Division « Hitlerjugend »*, Munin Verlag), Hubert Meyer note (p. 354, 2e éd., 1987) que la division ne perdit que 948 hommes dans la Poche de Falaise du 15 au 22 août (soit 45 tués, 248 blessés et 655 disparus). On est très loin de ce qui a pu être écrit, trop rapidement et sans vérification depuis plus de quarante ans : quelques chars et surtout quelques centaines de survivants seulement auraient échappé à l'enfer normand...

On a pris des chiffres concernant les arrière-gardes d'unités de couverture en croyant qu'ils correspondaient aux effectifs des divisions. Et cette erreur est devenue un cliché reproduit à l'infini. En ce qui concerne la *116. Panzer-Division*, elle dispose alors de 8 000 hommes à l'est de Vimoutiers, soit un total de 8 300 hommes et 12 chars.

Dans le tableau de la p. 114 de son article, M. Dufresne note tous les effectifs encore disponibles des deux armées allemandes engagées en Normandie : — 44 800 hommes sortis de la Poche, 60 000 hommes entre la mer et Gacé, 15 500 hommes entre Gacé et Nonancourt, 25 500 hommes entre Nonancourt et la Seine, 12 000 hommes à l'est de Vimoutiers, soit un total de 157 800 hommes se trouvant encore en Normandie. Les restes de la *Panzer-Lehr-Division*, soit 8 000 hommes, sont rassemblés près de Senlis. Ainsi, le 21 août, un total de **165 800 hommes** ayant combattu en Normandie est encore disponible pour le haut-commandement allemand. Mais beaucoup de matériel a été perdu. La *5. Panzerarmee* n'aligne plus qu'une petite centaine de panzers (entre 92 et 99), soit moins que la dotation d'une panzer-division alors qu'il sont répartis entre neuf divisions blindées et deux bataillons de chars lourds. Par ailleurs, au nord de la Seine, la *15. Armee* aligne un total de 72 000 hommes (soit 35 000 hommes près de la Seine et 37 000 hommes dans le Nord).

Tandis que les Allemands sortent leurs troupes encerclées de la Poche de Falaise, que font les Alliés ? Le groupement du général Patton rassemblant des divisions du *XV th Corps (5 th Armored Division, 79 th Infantry Division)* et du *XX th Corps (7 th Armored Division, 5 th Infantry Division)* est arrivé sur une ligne

Dreux, Nogent-le-Roi, Maintenon, en date du 16 août. Selon le plan initial, les Alliés devaient bloquer les Allemands sur la Seine. La formation de la Poche de Falaise avait été un « accident » non prévu et qui serait exploité comme l'on sait. Alors que le « court encerclement » de Falaise-Argentan est en train de s'achever, Montgomery met au point le « grand encerclement ». Le 19 août, le général Montgomery rassemble pour une conférence Bradley, Hodges (1re Armée US), Crerar (*First Canadian Army*) et Dempsey (*Second British Army*). Il manque un chef d'armée, celui de la *Third US Army*, le général Patton. Ce jour là il est enfin arrivé sur la Seine près de Mantes à la tête de son *XV th Corps*. Les Alliés décident alors d'envoyer des divisions le long de la Seine à l'Ouest de Mantes. Mais les unités britanniques sont trop éloignées de cet objectif et Bradley propose d'utiliser des unités américaines pour remplir cette mission. Elles obliqueront vers le nord-ouest dans le secteur attribué aux Britanniques. A la page 116 de son article, M. Dufresne note : « *Le programme était donc clairement tracé et les tâches bien réparties entre les Alliés. Montgomery et Bradley confirmèrent par écrit leur décisions. Il faut remarquer toutefois que la directive M 519 de Montgomery du 20 août prévoyait qu'au-delà d'Elbeuf les Américains enverraient des éléments légers vers l'estuaire de la Seine, ce que ne mentionnait pas la lettre d'Instructions n° 5 de Bradley du 19 août* ». Bradley affecte deux corps d'armée (le *XV th Corps* et le *XIX th Corps*) avec cinq divisions. Il engage ainsi des moyens plus importants que ceux qui étaient prévus. Le *XV th Corps* devra progresser jusqu'à Louviers et créer une tête de pont à Mantes. Le *XIX th Corps* devra avancer plus à l'ouest, entre Elbeuf et Louviers. Bradley engage des forces importantes dans cette mission mais, par ailleurs, il donne au général Patton le feu vert pour engager des divisions vers Melun, Fontainebleau et Sens. De nouveau, les Américains dispersent leurs moyens et sont surtout fascinés par une autre direction : l'Est et l'Allemagne. La Normandie est pour eux une affaire qui semble classée.

Du côté allemand, le maréchal von Kluge a été relevé de ses fonctions. Amer et déprimé, il se suicide. Un chef énergique, le maréchal Model, l'homme des situations désespérées, est nommé à sa place. Il planifie dès le 19 août un repli en bon ordre sur la Seine. Il déplace des divisions, fait établir des lignes défensives et prévoit un décrochage sur la Seine en quatre étapes.

Le **22 août**, la *5 th Armored Division* arrive dans l'est de l'Eure. Pacy-sur-Eure et Saint-Aquilin-de-Pacy sur la

Page ci-contre : **La retraite allemande au-delà de la Seine (du 21 au 30 août 1944).** Les Allemands se replient progressivement. Une partie du cours de la Risle sert de solide point d'ancrage pendant deux jours (26 et 27 août). Des soldats de groupements tactiques (comme le *SS-Panzer-Grenadier-Regiment « Hohenstaufen »*, autour de Brionne) retardent considérablement la pression alliée tandis que leurs camarades franchissent la Seine. Le plus gros point de passage est à **Rouen** où passeront environ 50 000 hommes. Le deuxième point de passage est à **Poses** (au nord de Louviers). Notons ensuite **Duclair** (point de passage de la division « Hohenstaufen »), **Caudebec-en-Caux** en aval de Duclair, mais aussi **Petit-Couronne, Elbeuf**, et de multiples points de passage avec des bacs légers qui assurent le transfert des hommes à pied et des véhicules hippomobiles (carte H. Fürbringer/Heimdal).

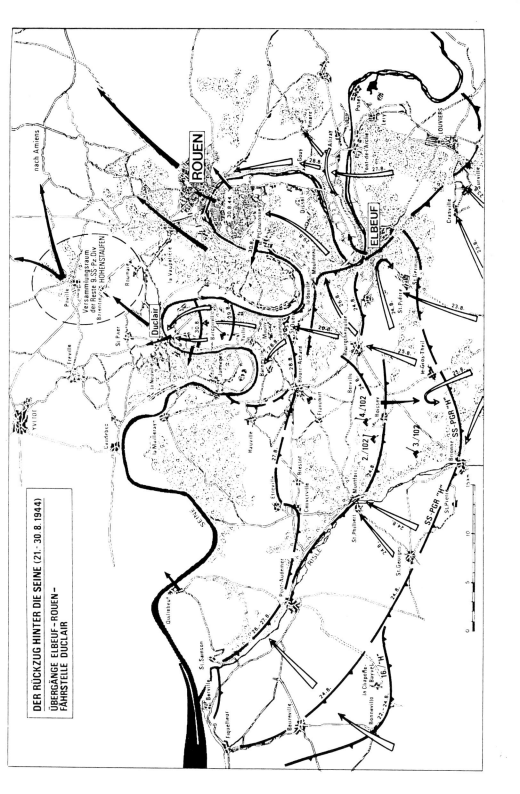

DER RÜCKZUG HINTER DIE SEINE (21.- 30. 8. 1944)

ÜBERGÄNGE ELBEUF – ROUEN – FÄHRSTELLE DUCLAIR

droite, Evreux au centre, Conches sur la gauche, sont atteints et dépassés. En face, il y a des éléments de la *116. Panzer-Division* devant Le Neubourg et des éléments de la *12. SS-Panzer-Division « Hitlerjugend »* en avant de Louviers. Plus à l'est, les Américains ont établi une tête de pont au nord de la Seine à partir de Mantes en repoussant, avec la *79 th Infantry Division*, les Allemands de la *49. Infanterie-Division*. Les Américains tiennent aussi Vernon maintenant. Sur tout le front entre Le Neubourg et Vernon, les Américains ont attaqué avec plusieurs centaines de chars, mais les Allemands se sont défendus avec acharnement. La division blindée américaine perd aujourd'hui 25 chars Sherman. Alors que les Américains progressent dans cette partie de la Normandie, les Allemands décrochent face aux Britanniques en se servant des rivières qui forment des vallées légèrement encaissées courant du sud au nord et constituant des lignes de repli idéales. Ils décrochent tout d'abord sur la Touques et les troupes de Montgomery ont pénétré dans Lisieux. La Risle permettra d'établir la denière ligne défensive avant la Seine.

Le **23 août**, le général Patton s'intéresse subitement à l'idée d'un « grand encerclement », comme le note M. Dufresne (p. 117, art.). Il veut faire passer deux corps d'armée entre Melun et Montereau, pour obliquer au nord de Paris vers Beauvais où les Allemands seraient bloqués. Le général Bradley ne répondra pas à sa proposition. Les Américains avancent faiblement autour d'Evreux face à une résistance allemande tenace. La division « Hitlerjugend » a établi quelques éléments devant Louviers en arc de cercle, en s'appuyant sur les forêts qui entourent la localité. Légèrement plus à l'ouest, les éléments de la *116. Panzer-Division* qui s'accrochent au Neubourg sont contraints de décrocher légèrement sur Amfréville-la-Campagne. Les gains américains de la journée restent très faibles. Plus à l'ouest, les Canadiens de la *First Canadian Army* ont atteint la Risle et l'ont dépassé en quelques endroits. Tandis que des éléments de couverture allemands freinent l'assaut allié, le franchissement de la Seine se fait de manière intensive, jour et nuit. Montgomery avait pensé que la destruction de la plupart des ponts sur la Seine aurait bloqué les Allemands devant le grand fleuve. Le franchissement se fait sur des ponts non détruits ou remis en état à Rouen et à Elbeuf mais aussi sur un grand nombre de bacs de diverses tailles (voir en encadré l'extrait de l'ouvrage de Herbert Fürbringer sur la division « Hohenstaufen » décrivant le franchissement de la Seine près de Duclair par cette division). Des dizaines de milliers de soldats en retraite vont franchir la Seine ces prochains jours.

Le **24 août**, les Canadiens resserrent leur étreinte et arrivent devant Bourgthéroulde, un important nœud routier au sud de la Seine. Les Américains avancent faiblement devant Elbeuf et Louviers. Les divisions américaines du *XIX th Corps* devaient affronter un adversaire démoralisé par les revers et elles ont mis en fait quatre jours pour avancer de 80 kilomètres et, ces deux derniers jours, la progression est faible.

A partir du **25 août**, les Allemands vont se replier progressivement sur les boucles de la Seine où ont lieu les principales traversées du fleuve. Le franchissement de la Seine va se poursuivre les **26, 27 et 28 août**. L'opération est terminée le **29 août**. Les Allemands ont abandonné 4 000 véhicules, pour la plupart détruits par les chasseurs-bombardiers alliés. Mais **165 000 hommes** ont franchi la Seine sur 25 000 véhicules. Michel Dufresne tire ainsi le bilan de cette opération (p. 117 art. cité) : « *L'ensemble des troupes retirées représentait environ les trois quarts des effectifs allemands présents en Normandie au début du mois d'août. Les huit divisions d'infanterie prises dans la Poche avaient sauvé seulement*

*16 % de leur effectif nominal au début de juin. Les huit divisions non encerclées avaient sauvé 67 % de leur effectif. L'ensemble des divisions de panzers et la division panzer-grenadier avaient retiré 53 % de leur effectif nominal* ». A la page 119 de son article, Michel Dufresne publie un fort intéressant tableau. Nous y apprenons que sur un effectif nominal de 371 000 hommes (soit vingt neuf divisions), 165 300 hommes ont repassé la Seine, soit 67 000 hommes pour les divisions d'infanterie et de parachutistes et 98 300 hommes pour les divisions blindées. Il faut noter que sept divisions d'infanterie (les 276e, 326e, 344e, 346e, 363e, 708e, 711e) avaient des effectifs nominaux faibles, soit 8 000 hommes, mais trois d'entre elles alignent encore 6 000 hommes après le franchissement de la Seine (soit les trois quarts de l'effectif nominal).

En ce qui concerne les divisions blindées, les effectifs restent en général élevés : la *1. SS-Panzer-Division* compte 10 000 hommes, 12 000 hommes pour la *2. SS-Panzer-Division*, 15 000 hommes pour la *9. SS-Panzer-Division*, 10 000 hommes pour la *10. SS-Panzer-Division*, 12 000 hommes pour la *12. SS-Panzer-Division*, 6 000 hommes pour la *17. SS-Panzer-grenadier-Division*, 8 000 hommes pour la *2. Panzer-Division*, 1 000 hommes pour la *9. Panzer-Division* (mais cette division n'avait pu en totalité rejoindre le front de Normandie), 8 000 hommes pour la *21. Panzer-Division*, 8 300 hommes pour la *116. Panzer-Division*, 8 000 hommes pour la *Panzer-Lehr-Division*. Par contre, quatre divisions d'infanterie ont particulièrement souffert, chacune d'elles ne ramenant qu'un millier d'hommes (sur un effectif initial de 8 000 hommes toutefois, sauf pour la première cité qui en comptait 14 000) : les 84e, 326e, 363e et 708e.

## Le bilan

Ainsi, les Allemands ont subi des pertes importantes dans la Poche de Falaise mais ils ont pu sauver plus de la moitié des troupes qui avaient été encerclées. Malgré de nouvelles pertes, causées en très grande partie par l'aviation alliée, les Allemands perdent encore de nombreux véhicules mais sauvent la grande majorité de leurs hommes. Pour eux, la fin de la Bataille de Normandie est en quelque sorte un « Dunkerque allemand ». A l'annonce du succès du franchissement de la Seine par les Allemands, Winston Churchill est atterré. On lui avait dit que les Allemands ne pourraient franchir le grand fleuve normand car tous les ponts étaient détruits. Et pourtant ils l'ont fait. Il crée une commission d'enquête. Celle-ci note, comme le rappelle M. Dufresne, que les Allemands « *avaient utilisé un pont de chemin de fer à Rouen, un pont flottant à Elbeuf, un autre à Louviers et une multitude de moyens de fortune ; soixante points de franchissement avaient été dénombrés. Cette opération avait surtout été effectuée de nuit. Les forêts bordant la Seine sur ses deux rives, les nombreux méandres décrits par le fleuve, le mauvais temps qui sévit plusieurs jours et la présence de batteries anti-aériennes avaient favorisé sa réalisation* ». La RAF a même établi un rapport précis avec une carte de la Seine donnant des détails sur les divers points de franchissement.

Les Allemands se sont repliés en ordre et avec discipline ce qui leur a permis d'échapper au désastre. Des chefs expérimentés et énergiques ont dirigé les opérations de repli : le maréchal Model, le General Hausser et le General Eberbach. Alors que Model se chargeait de recevoir et remettre en route les unités qui sortaient de la Poche, Hausser se trouvait au milieu de ses hommes dans l'enfer de la Poche pour les entraîner vers la sortie. Par la suite Model, comme nous l'avons vu, planifie le repli sur la Seine. Ensuite, dès le **30 août**, il reconstitue un front cohérent au nord du fleuve (comme nous le montre une carte d'état-major de l'époque). Il prévoit une ligne de repli sur la Somme. Les armées de Normandie décrocheront ensuite, avec la 15e Armée, vers la Belgique.

Les Allemands ont perdu beaucoup d'hommes mais ils ont sauvé la majorité d'entre eux. Ils ont perdu la plus grande partie de leur matériel mais ils pourront en remplacer la plus grande part. C'est à l'été de 1944 que la production allemande de blindés et d'avions atteint des sommets (la différence réside dans le fait que la production de guerre américaine atteint de « fantastiques » sommets). Ils pourront donc compenser en grande partie les pertes en matériel. Par contre, il aurait été quasiment impossible de compenser les pertes en hommes si les Alliés avaient capturé 100 000 à 150 000 hommes (cela était possible si un double encerclement avait été effectivement lancé à partir du 12 août). Parmi les dizaines de milliers d'hommes qui se sont échappés, il y a avait des généraux, des officiers d'état-major et des cadres dont la perte était totalement irremplaçable. Quant aux sous-officiers et hommes de troupe, ils étaient très expérimentés, aguerris. Il aurait été difficile de les remplacer. D'ailleurs, lorsque les divisions blindées sorties de Normandie furent reconstituées pour être mises en ligne au moment de l'offensive des Ardennes, le haut-commandement préleva des hommes de la Kriegsmarine et des rampants de la Luftwaffe pour combler les vides. Ces hommes disposaient d'une instruction militaire mais pas d'une formation de combattants. Il ne fut pas possible d'en faire des « soldats » en quelques semaines. Leur apport fit chuter la qualité militaire des divisions concernées. On le verra lors de l'offensive de Ardennes. La « levée en masse » est une illusion dans une guerre moderne. Il faut des mois, sinon des années, pour faire un bon soldat. Les divisions allemandes, qui avaient été engagées en Normandie, ont survécu pour la plupart d'entre elles parce que l'essentiel avait été conservé. Les Alliés les retrouveront sur leur chemin dans les mois à venir. Le 17 septembre, les paras britanniques sautent sur Arnhem. Le succès est pour Montgomery à portée de la main. Il est aux portes de la Ruhr. Mais que trouvent-ils en face d'eux ? Les paras sont battus par des vétérans allemands des divisions « Hohenstaufen » et « Frundsberg » qui se sont repliés de Normandie. C'est un échec pour les Britanniques. Le 16 décembre 1944, Hitler lance l'offensive des Ardennes, elle menace dangereusement les Alliés pendant quelques jours. Toutes les divisions blindées engagées sont des divisions rescapées de la Normandie. Plus de la moitié des effectifs — et les meilleurs — sont des vétérans du front de Normandie. Il est évident que si la victoire alliée en Normandie avait permis de prendre au piège l'essentiel des divisions allemandes qui s'y trouvaient, cette victoire eut été un triomphe. La guerre se serait probablement terminée vers la fin du mois d'octobre. La guerre aurait été raccourcie de plus de six mois.

Mais comment les Alliés ont-ils laissé échapper la chance d'une victoire totale et définitive pourtant à portée de leur main ? Tout d'abord, les Allemands bénéficient d'un important avantage. Ils disposent du meilleur corps d'officiers du monde. Leurs généraux et leurs officiers d'état-major sont très bien formés. ils disposent en outre d'une expérience de plus de quatre ans de guerre. Certains d'entre eux sont des officiers brillants qui savent prendre des mesures rapides et énergiques en situation de crise. Quant aux combattants, la plupart d'entre eux sont expérimentés et endurants. Les Américains ont dû former rapidement leurs soldats et leurs officiers. Ces derniers sont instruits en quatre-vingt dix jours (les « Ninety days wonders ») et la bonne volonté compense rarement l'expérience. Par ailleurs, les officiers généraux et les officiers d'état-major manquent eux-aussi d'expérience. Seul Montgomery, le vainqueur d'El Alamein, dispose d'une expérience équivalente à celle des grands chefs allemands comme Eberbach. Le deuxième point faible des Alliés doit être recherché dans le système de commandement. La coalition de deux grandes nations ne facilite pas la cohésion du commandement et, comme nous l'avons vu, Montgomery n'était pas toujours tenu au courant des initiatives de ses alliés et subordonnés. Bien plus, ses ordres n'étaient pas toujours appliqués.

A un moment où la vitesse et la rapidité de décision devaient décider du sort de la guerre, comme le note M. Dufresne (art. cité p. 118) : « (Bradley) *adopte avec Montgomery une attitude conforme à leurs liens hiérarchiques, mais ce n'est qu'une façade. Initiateur de l'encerclement entre Argentan et Falaise, il dégarnit le secteur d'Argentan à l'insu de Montgomery. Il disperse ensuite ses troupes le jour où il reçoit l'ordre de les concentrer vers la Seine(...). En conséquence, à Falaise, la tâche d'assurer la fermeture de la poche revient presque exclusivement aux Canadiens qui s'embrouillent, ne s'engagent pas suffisamment et laissent une brèche ouverte. Sur la Seine, répétition en quelque sorte de ce qui s'est passé à Falaise, les unités américaines chargées d'interdire l'accès du fleuve aux Allemands ne s'engagent pas avec vigueur et la mission échoue ».* Et, pourtant les Alliés disposaient alors d'une supériorité de quarante contre un pour l'aviation et de huit contre un pour les chars (après la Bataille de Mortain), cette supériorité en chars passe à quarante contre un après la sortie de la Poche de Falaise. Après le brillant succès américain de l'Opération Cobra et de son exploitation, le fonctionnement du commandement allié a laissé des grains de sable s'introduire dans la formidable machine de guerre alliée. Il est facile, quarante-cinq ans après, d'étudier par le menu les raisons d'une « victoire inachevée », mais tout ceci nous rappelle que le hasard, l'enchaînement des circonstances, un retard qui entraîne un autre, peuvent changer le cours des événements et retarder, dans le cas précis, la victoire finale de près de sept mois.

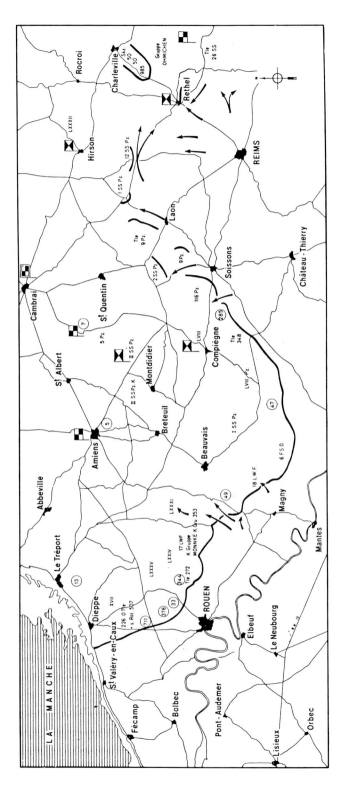

**Le Groupe d'Armées B rétablit une nouvelle ligne de front au nord de la Seine à partir du 30 août** (carte établie d'après un document allemand). On note la présence sur la ligne de front d'unités qui ont combattu en Normandie : des divisions d'infanterie comme la 711e et la 344e, la 6e Fallschirmjäger-Division, la 17e Luftwaffen-Felddivision, des divisions blindées comme la 116e, la 9e, la 2e SS, la 1re SS, la 12e SS.

Achevé d'imprimer sur les presses de l'Imprimerie YVERT à Amiens pour le compte des Editions
Heimdal à Bayeux
Dépôt légal : juin 1992 (22652)